Aging:
The
Ethnic
Factor

Little, Brown Series on Gerontology

Series Editors	Jon Hendricks and Robert Kastenbaum	
Published	Donald E. Gelfand *Aging: The Ethnic Factor* Jennie Keith *Old People As People: Social and Cultural Influences on Aging and Old Age*	Theodore Koff *Long-Term Care: An Approach to Serving the Frail Elderly*
Forthcoming Titles	W. Andrew Achenbaum *Aging: History and Ideology* Linda M. Breytspraak *The Development of Self in Later Life* Carroll Estes *Political Economy, Health, and Aging* Charles Harris et al. *Applied Research In Aging* C. Davis Hendricks *Law and Aging*	John L. Horn *Aging and Adult Development of Cognitive Functions* John F. Myles *Political Economy of Pensions* Martha Storandt *Counseling and Psychotherapy* Albert J. E. Wilson III *Social Services For Older Persons*

Aging: The Ethnic Factor

Donald E. Gelfand
University of Maryland at Baltimore

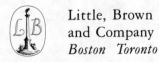

Little, Brown
and Company
Boston Toronto

Library of Congress Cataloging
in Publication Data

Gelfand, Donald E.
  Aging, The Ethnic Factor.
  Includes bibliographies and index.
    1. Minority   aged—United   States.   2.
Ethnicity—United   States.   3.   Aging—United
States. 4. Aged—United States.
I. Title.
HQ1064.U5G38   305.2'6   81-14786
ISBN 0–316–307130   AACR2
ISBN 0–316–307149 (pbk.)

Book design by Harold Pattek

Library of Congress Catalog Card No. 81–14786

ISBN 0–316–307130
ISBN 0–316–307149 (pbk.)

9 8 7 6 5 4 3 2 1

HAL

Published simultaneously in Canada
by Little, Brown & Company (Canada) Limited

Printed in the United States of America

Contents

Foreword
to
Series

Where is it? In each of the billions of cells in our bodies? Or in our minds? Then, again, perhaps it is something that happens *between* people. Ought not we to take a look at the marketplace as well? And at the values expressed through our cultural institutions? Undoubtedly, the answer certainly lies in all of these factors — and others. The phenomenon of aging takes place within our bodies, in our minds, between ourselves and others, and as culturally defined patterns.

Burgeoning as the field is, the study and analysis of aging is deserving of an integrated spectrum approach. Now, Little, Brown and Company offers such a perspective, one designed to respond to the diversity and complexity of the subject matter and to individualized instructional needs. The Little, Brown Series on Gerontology provides a series of succinct and readable books that encompass a wide variety of topics and concerns. Each volume, written by a highly qualified gerontologist, will provide a degree of precision and specificity not available in a general text whose coverage, expertise, and interest level cannot help but be uneven. While the scope of the gerontology series is indeed broad, individual volumes provide accurate, up-to-date presentations unmatched in the literature of gerontology.

The Little, Brown Series on Gerontology:

—provides a comprehensive overview
—explores emerging challenges and extends the frontiers of knowledge
—is organically interrelated via cross-cutting themes
—consists of individual volumes prepared by the most qualified experts
—offers maximum flexibility as teaching materials
—insures manageable length without sacrificing concepts, facts, methods, or issues.

With the Little, Brown Series on Gerontology now becoming available, instructors can select the exact mix of texts most desirable for their individual courses. Practitioners and other professionals will also find the foundations necessary to remain abreast of their own particular areas. No doubt students, too, will respond to the knowledge and enthusiasm of gerontologists writing about those topics they know and care most about.

Little, Brown and Company and the editors are pleased to provide a series that not only looks at conceptual and theoretical questions but squarely addresses the most critical and applied concerns of the 1980s. Knowledge without action is unacceptable. The reverse is no better.

As the list of volumes makes clear, some books focus primarily on research and theoretical concerns, others on the applied; by this two-sided approach they draw upon the most significant and dependable thinking available. It is to be hoped that they will serve as a wellspring for developments in years to come.

Acknowledgments

As the reader will quickly see, the literature and knowledge about ethnicity and aging is hardly definitive. In pulling together what we know about this field into some reasonable coherence, I have been assisted by a number of individuals: Judy Gelfand, who always allows me to use her as a sounding board for my ideas about topics and never shirks from reading my chapter drafts; Jon Hendricks and Bob Kastenbaum, the general editors of this series who have provided valuable comments as the writing progressed; and George Bergquist and Herbert Nolan at Winthrop Publishers who guided the book from the beginning stages to final production. As is true of all authors, I must take responsibility for the views expressed throughout the book.

D.E.G.

Aging:
The
Ethnic
Factor

Introduction

The
Study
of Ethnicity

The study of ethnicity in the United States has a number of unique rewards. Focusing on ethnicity provides an understanding of the composite social and political attitudes that are prevalent in contemporary America. It also brings us into contact with a group of older persons whose historical experiences have been distinctive.

Aged blacks are individuals whose lives may have spanned the major historical changes in the South, including those following Reconstruction, the large migration of blacks from the South to the North, and the race riots that have marred this century. While these elderly black men and women did not live in slavery, it is still fresh in their minds as recounted by their parents. They are thus an important link to a crucial period of American history. Similar historical events have characterized the lives of elderly Mexican-Americans and Asian-Americans. Both groups can discuss from personal experience the problems of attempting to develop a life for themselves in a country that regarded them as useful for manual labor but inappropriate as neighbors.

Among whites, the generation of older people in their eighties and nineties represents the last group of individuals who could have been part of the massive European immigration to this country during the 1800s and early 1900s. This extensive immigration by diverse cultures will never recur in equal variety or numbers. A unique historical resource will disappear with the present generation of aged white and nonwhite ethnic groups unless oral and written histories of their experiences are now prepared.

Besides providing the researcher with a connection to

important periods of American history, the study of ethnicity and aging holds out the promise of revealing some hitherto unknown secrets about longevity. It is now believed that genetics are a major determinant of an individual's life expectancy. The question is how much of a person's life expectancy is genetically determined and how much is influenced by personality and behavior. The study of older individuals with varied genetic backgrounds and varied personality configurations which may be related to ethnic culture provides us with an opportunity to gain some important knowledge about these questions.

While exploring determinants of life expectancy may be provocative, a number of other issues are addressed by the study of ethnicity and aging. They include a greater understanding of the family as a unit. Our examination of ethnicity and aging allows us to focus intensely on the basic elements that bind families together and the types of assistance and relationships between generations that are most important in maintaining family units. It also sheds light on other basic questions, including how members of various ethnic groups approach growing older, how they attempt to meet the changes that are associated with old age, what factors are most important in producing satisfaction with the later years of their lives, and how they regard the prospect of eventual death.

Beyond the importance that the answers to these questions hold for any understanding of aging are significant implications for the provision of services to both aged members of ethnic groups and their families. Cultural variables may affect the willingness of individuals from various ethnic groups to use services, regardless of need. The study of ethnicity and aging allows us to relate the use of services to the cultural backgrounds of older adults, their historical experiences in the United States, and especially their past experiences with services. In this sense, the exploration of ethnicity and aging is crucial to the continued development of programs and services that both meet the needs of older persons and are utilized by those from distinctive ethnic backgrounds.

We can best translate this relatively abstract discussion into concrete terms by examining the importance of ethnicity for three older individuals.

Mr. X is seventy-two years old. Before retiring seven years ago, he worked for a steel company as a manual laborer, a position he had occupied for twenty-five years. His major nonwork interests centered around spectator sports and television. His wife, to whom he had been married for thirty years, died five years ago. Mr. X and his wife were not active in any organizations and had only a small circle of friends. Mr. X now spends his time watching television and reading sports magazines. He lives in a clean one-bedroom apartment, cooks his own meals, and takes care of the apartment himself.

He sees or speaks to his children approximately once every eight weeks and rarely sees friends. He rarely goes out to any social events. He has mild hypertension and a 40 percent hearing loss which is job-related.

Mrs. Y is seventy-eight years old. She moved to Florida from Philadelphia four years ago. Before moving she devoted herself to raising her children and taking care of the large family home. When her husband died six years ago, she began to become involved in a number of activities. After moving to Florida she took a part-time job serving food in a cafeteria. She complains of fatigue from her job. At night she goes out to clubs and to parties held in the retirement village where she lives. While she speaks to her children at least once a month, she only sees them once a year, when she travels north during the summer. At those times she seems restless and complains of being away from the day-long activities she usually undertakes. Her medical problems have included removal of a gall bladder, a mastectomy, and severe depression after the death of her husband. Her only medications at present are over-the-counter drugs.

Mrs. Z is eighty-two years old. Her physical health has been deteriorating in the last few years and she now suffers from a number of problems, including arteriosclerotic heart disease, mild chronic brain syndrome, and diabetes controlled by diet. She takes a number of medications to control her physical condition. Until recently Mrs. Z was active in many organizations, including the local block organization, church groups, and a hospital group. She continued these activities after her husband died in 1969. During the last three years she has had to abandon some of these activities, and she is finding it hard to keep her one-bedroom apartment clean as well as cook her meals. She is also finding it hard to engage in any extra activities because of her limited financial resources. She sees or talks to her children at least once a week.

All three of these individuals are familiar to service providers. While it might be easy to understand the need for Mrs. Z to cut down her activities because of her physical condition, we cannot explain her attitude toward her health and the behaviors and attitudes of the other two individuals without raising a number of questions about the effects of a large number of variables, including ethnicity. The questions we could ask about the impact of these three individuals' ethnic backgrounds include:

Does Mrs. Z's ethnic background help to explain her relationships with her children?

Does her ethnic background also provide a clue to her involvement with organizations?

How much of Mr. X's interest in sports or his relationships with friends can be explained by his ethnic background?

Would Mrs. Y's move to Florida be different in meaning for an individual from one ethnic background rather than another?

Could Mrs. Y's continued interest in working be explained in part by the attitudes toward work common among her ethnic group?

To what extent can the ethnic background of any of these individuals be important in understanding the type of assistance they might want, or even accept, from family, friends, or formal service providers?

Might the ethnic background of these individuals be a crucial factor in planning approaches to interesting them in a variety of programs and activities for older adults?

Unfortunately, answering these questions is difficult because our understanding of ethnicity and aging is limited. There is only limited agreement on terminology and only limited knowledge about the influence of ethnicity, however defined, on the lives of individuals. Not surprisingly, this ambiguity is also true in the area of ethnicity and aging. The major trend among researchers has been to view elderly people as a homogeneous group in which age is a leveler of all other characteristics. All aging individuals face certain changes that they must deal with, but it is not clear that everyone attempts to cope with these changes in the same manner. Age may be only one of the factors that affect how individuals deal with changes in their lives. Other factors include sex, socioeconomic background, family relationships, living situation, physical condition, and ethnicity.

In the past, the field of gerontology has often ignored all of these variables in its desire to prove the importance of age. Indeed, many of the effects of age may have been overstated in an often frenzied attempt to draw attention to older adults as a group in need of distinct programs and services. While many elderly people are still underserved, there has been an immense growth of programs and services in aging since the passage of the Older Americans Act in 1965.

It is now possible, and indeed necessary, to reflect on the complexity that surrounds growing older in American society. This reflection may help us not only gain an understanding of the basic processes of aging in all of their sociological, psychological, and biological manifestations, but also provide a critical base for evaluating the basic assumptions upon which many of the programs in aging are built. It is possible that many programs are overlooking important variables and are thus doomed to failure. A major factor in this regard is ethnicity. In mental health and health, a focus on ethnicity has already helped provide an understanding of some thorny service-delivery issues. It is hoped that this volume will sensitize all readers to the need to include ethnicity as a major variable in any sociological or psychological research or planning effort for aged citizens.

Undertaking an effort to synthesize an approach to aged members of ethnic groups involves some basic decision making. The first decision concerns the designation of the groups that we are going to include under the rubric "ethnic aged." The approach that we will use throughout this volume is to include all groups, either white or nonwhite, that are commonly termed ethnic or minority.

The second task is to decide whether we should advocate the importance of ethnicity in this society. Because of the heated debate that seems to accompany discussions about ethnicity, we will make every effort in this volume to work from data now available, drawing implications where the data are incomplete but always trying to stay within a conceptual framework that is grounded in data. The problem facing researchers is to define the differences among ethnic groups, what their meaning is for the lives of ethnic older people, and the degree to which these differences will continue to exist among future generations of aged.

Ethnic Groups in the United States

It is difficult to explore the wide diversity of ethnic groups in the United States without providing a long list of the groups and their numbers. Table 1, based on immigration figures, provides a reasonable summary of the major groups represented in the ethnic stock of this country.

Since the U.S. Bureau of the Census is forbidden to collect information on religion, it is hard to determine the religious preferences of each of these nationality and racial groups. As Weed concludes from his analysis of U.S. data: "If we define 'ethnic' as any 'individual who differs by religion, language and culture from the white Protestant Anglo-Saxon settlers,' the figure would exceed 65 percent of the total population" (1973, p. 12).

The numbers of elderly people among each of these groups also vary. Among minorities such as black and Spanish-heritage groups, the proportion of older adults has been lower than among whites because of higher mortality at younger ages and higher fertility rates. Thus only 8 percent of the black population, 4 percent of the Spanish-origin population, and 6 percent of native Americans are over sixty-five. In contrast, 11 percent of the total American population is over sixty-five.

While the proportion of elderly among recent immigrants

Table 1
Immigrants, by Country of Last Permanent Residence: 1820 to 1977

Country	1820–1977 total	1951–1960 total	1961–1970 total	1972	1973	1974	1975	1976	1977	Percent 1820–1977	Percent 1961–1970	Percent 1971–1977
Total	47,960	2,515.5	3,321.7	384.7	400.1	394.9	386.2	398.6	462.3	100.0	100.0	100.0
Europe	36,108	1,325.6	1,123.4	86.3	91.2	80.4	72.8	73.0	74.0	75.3	33.8	20.4
Austria[a]	4,314	67.1	20.6	2.3	1.6	.7	.5	.5	.5	8.9	.6	.3
Hungary		36.6	5.4	.5	1.0	.9	.6	.6	.5		.2	.2
Belgium	202	18.6	9.2	.5	.4	.4	.4	.5	.5	.4	.3	.1
Czechoslovakia	137	.9	3.3	1.2	.9	.4	.3	.3	.3	.3	.1	.2
Denmark	364	11.0	9.2	.5	.4	.5	.3	.4	.4	.8	.3	.1
Finland	33	4.9	4.2	.3	.3	.2	.2	.2	.2	.1	.1	.1
France	747	51.1	45.2	2.9	2.6	2.2	1.8	2.0	2.7	1.6	1.4	.6
Germany[a]	6,968	477.8	190.8	7.8	7.6	7.2	5.9	6.6	7.4	14.5	5.7	1.8
Great Britain[b]	4,879	195.5	210.0	11.5	11.9	11.7	12.2	13.0	14.0	10.2	6.3	3.1
Greece	646	47.6	86.0	10.5	10.3	10.6	9.8	8.6	7.8	1.3	2.6	2.6
Ireland[c]	4,722	57.3	37.5	1.4	1.6	1.3	1.1	1.0	1.0	9.9	1.1	.3
Italy	5,285	185.5	214.1	22.4	22.3	15.0	11.0	8.0	7.4	11.0	6.4	3.9
Netherlands	358	52.3	30.6	1.0	1.0	1.0	.8	.9	1.0	.8	.9	.2
Norway	856	22.9	15.5	.4	.4	.4	.4	.3	.3	1.8	.5	.1
Poland[a]	510	10.0	53.5	3.8	4.1	3.5	3.5	3.2	3.3	1.1	1.6	.8
Portugal	432	19.6	76.1	9.5	10.0	10.7	11.3	11.0	10.0	.9	2.3	2.6
Spain	254	7.9	44.7	4.3	5.5	4.7	2.6	2.8	5.6	.5	1.3	1.0
Sweden	1,271	21.7	17.1	.7	.6	.6	.5	.6	.6	2.7	.6	.2
Switzerland	348	17.7	18.5	1.0	.7	.7	.7	.8	.8	.7	.6	.2
USSR[a,d]	3,367	.6	2.3	.4	.9	.9	4.7	7.4	5.4	7.0	.1	.7
Yugoslavia	111	8.2	20.4	2.8	5.2	5.0	2.9	2.3	2.3	.2	.6	.9
Other Europe	304	10.8	9.2	.6	1.9	1.8	1.3	2.0	2.0	.6	.3	.4

Table 1 (continued)

Country	1820–1977 total	1951–1960 total	1961–1970 total	1972	1973	1974	1975	1976	1977	Percent 1820–1977	Percent 1961–1970	Percent 1971–1977
Asia	2,573	153.3	427.8	116.0	120.0	127.0	129.2	146.7	150.8	5.4	12.9	31.7
China[e]	510	9.7	34.8	8.5	9.2	10.0	9.2	9.9	12.5	1.0	1.0	2.4
Hong Kong[f]	169	15.5	75.0	10.9	10.3	10.7	12.5	13.7	12.3	.4	2.3	2.8
India	140	2.0	27.2	15.6	12.0	11.7	14.3	16.1	16.8	.3	.8	3.5
Iran[f]	33	3.4	10.3	2.9	2.9	2.5	2.2	2.6	4.2	.1	.3	.7
Israel[f]	80	25.5	29.6	3.0	2.9	2.9	3.5	5.2	4.4	.2	.9	.8
Japan	400	46.3	40.0	5.0	6.1	5.4	4.8	4.8	4.5	.8	1.2	1.3
Jordan[f]	34	5.8	11.7	2.4	2.1	2.5	2.3	2.4	2.9	.1	.3	.6
Korea[f]	211	6.2	34.5	18.1	22.3	27.5	28.1	30.6	30.7	.4	1.0	6.1
Lebanon[f]	46	4.5	15.2	3.0	2.6	3.0	4.0	5.0	5.5	.1	.5	.9
Philippines[g]	343	19.3	98.4	28.7	30.2	32.5	31.3	36.8	38.5	.7	3.0	8.1
Turkey	384	3.5	10.1	1.5	1.4	1.4	1.1	1.0	1.0	.8	.3	.3
Vietnam[h]	26	2.7	4.2	3.4	4.5	3.1	2.7	2.4	3.4	.1	.1	.8
Other Asia	197	9.0	36.7	13.0	13.5	13.8	13.2	16.2	14.1	.4	1.2	3.4
America	8,740	996.9	1,716.4	173.2	179.6	178.8	174.7	169.2	223.2	18.2	51.7	45.4
Argentina[i]	89	19.5	49.7	2.5	2.9	2.9	2.8	2.7	3.1	.2	1.5	.7
Brazil[i]	55	13.8	29.3	1.8	1.8	1.6	1.4	1.4	1.9	.1	.9	.4
Canada	4,077	378.0	413.3	18.6	14.8	12.3	11.2	11.4	18.0	8.5	12.4	3.9
Colombia[j]	133	18.0	72.0	5.2	5.3	5.9	6.4	5.7	8.2	.3	2.2	1.5
Cuba[j]	490	78.9	208.5	19.9	22.5	17.4	25.6	28.4	66.1	1.0	6.3	7.2
Dominican Rep.[i]	194	9.9	93.3	10.8	14.0	15.7	14.1	12.4	11.6	.4	2.8	3.2
Ecuador[i]	80	9.8	36.8	4.4	4.2	4.8	4.7	4.5	5.2	.2	1.1	1.2
El Salvador[i]	38	5.9	15.0	2.0	2.0	2.3	2.4	2.4	4.4	.1	.4	.6
Guatemala[i]	36	4.7	15.9	1.7	1.8	1.6	1.9	2.0	3.7	.1	.5	.5
Haiti[i]	76	4.4	34.5	5.5	4.6	3.8	5.0	5.3	5.2	.1	1.0	1.3
Honduras[i]	31	6.0	15.7	1.0	1.4	1.4	1.4	1.3	1.6	.1	.5	.3
Mexico	2,015	299.8	453.9	64.2	70.4	71.9	62.6	58.4	44.6	4.2	13.7	15.1

Table 1 (continued)

Country	1820–1977 total	1951–1960 total	1961–1970 total	1972	1973	1974	1975	1976	1977	Percent 1820–1977	Percent 1961–1970	Percent 1971–1977
Panama[i]	43	11.7	19.4	1.6	1.7	1.7	1.7	1.8	2.5	.1	.6	.5
Peru[i]	42	7.4	19.1	1.5	1.8	2.0	2.3	2.6	3.9	.1	.6	.6
West Indies	684	29.8	133.9	24.2	21.6	24.4	22.3	19.6	27.1	1.4	4.0	5.9
Other America	657	99.2	106.2	8.3	8.8	9.1	8.9	9.3	16.1	1.3	3.2	2.5
Africa	119	14.1	29.0	5.5	5.5	5.2	5.9	5.7	9.6	.3	.9	1.5
Australia and New Zealand	116	11.5	19.6	2.6	2.5	2.0	1.8	2.1	2.5	.2	.6	.6
All other	304	14.0	5.7	1.2	1.3	1.4	1.8	1.9	2.2	.6	.2	.4

Note: In thousands, except percent. Years end on June 30 until 1977, after which they end on September 30. Data prior to 1906 refer to country from which aliens came. Because of boundary changes and changes in list of countries separately reported, data for certain countries not comparable throughout.

[a] 1938–1945, Austria included with Germany; 1899–1919, Poland included with Austria-Hungary, Germany, and USSR.
[b] Beginning 1952, includes data for United Kingdom not specified, formerly included with Other Europe.
[c] Comprises Eire and Northern Ireland.
[d] Europe and Asia.
[e] Beginning 1957, includes Taiwan.
[f] Prior to 1951, included with Other Asia.
[g] Prior to 1951, Philippines included with All Other.
[h] Prior to 1953, data for Vietnam not available.
[i] Prior to 1951, included with Other America.
[j] Prior to 1951, included with West Indies.

Source: U.S. Immigration and Naturalization Service, annual reports.

also approximates the national figures, the elderly population is smaller among groups such as Indochinese who have recently come to the United States as refugees and among the large number of illegal aliens in the country. Blacks comprise the fastest growing group of ethnic older persons. The black aged over sixty-five increased 28 percent between 1970 and 1978 in comparison to an increase of 19 percent among whites over 65. Among both blacks and whites the number of women over sixty-five far exceeds the number of men. In 1980 there were 148 white women over sixty-five for every 100 white men. Among blacks over 65 there were 141 women for every 100 men (Williams 1980).

Approximately one-third of both black and white elderly are living alone, but 29 percent of elderly black families are headed by women as compared to only 11 percent of elderly white families. In contrast we find that 18 percent of Hispanic elderly over fifty-five live alone in comparison to 24 percent of the United States population over the age of fifty-five (Torres-Gil and Negm 1980). Although often discussed as one group, it is important for us to note that Hispanics comprise a number of major ethnic groups. Mexican-Americans make up 60 percent of Hispanics in the United States, Puerto Ricans 14 percent, Cubans 6 percent, and individuals from Central or South America and Europe the remaining 20 percent (Torres-Gil and Negm 1980).

Besides varying in their proportions of older individuals, ethnic groups are unequally distributed throughout the United States. They have clustered in specific regions, rather than being randomly distributed. This clustering has been important, since it has allowed group members to preserve and pass on the ethnic culture from one generation to another.

American Indians are residents of areas primarily west of the Mississippi. Migration from the South has reduced the numbers of blacks living in that region and increased the representation of blacks in all metropolitan areas. In fact, only 53 percent of all blacks but 60 percent of blacks over 65 now live in the South (Williams 1980). Among Latin groups, Mexican-Americans are still represented most heavily in the Southwest and California, while Puerto Ricans have clustered in major industrial cities, particularly New York and Chicago. Asian-Americans remain predominantly a West Coast population, but Chinatowns and other Oriental communities can also be found in many American cities, including Boston and New York.

The major concentration of white ethnic groups is on the East Coast and in middle western cities that offered excellent work opportunities for immigrants in the late 1800s. Poles, for example, comprise a large proportion of the population of cities such as Buffalo, Baltimore, Chicago, and Gary. Fifty percent of all Italian-

Americans live within two hundred miles of New York City, especially in some of the cities of New England (Wallechinsky and Wallace 1979). Because of the high proportion of southern and eastern Europeans, the Catholic and Jewish representation in these cities is also strong.

Many ethnic groups and their elderly members are living in dense ethnic communities within central cities. Discussing blacks, for example, a recent report notes:

> Estimates indicate that the number of black older persons living in central cities will double by about 1990; the projected increase for older white persons is only three percent. Thus, older blacks may come to constitute one-fourth of the population of our central cities, instead of the 16 percent which they represented in the early 1970s. (Urban Resources Consultants 1978, p. 11)

Eighty-one percent of Mexican-Americans also live in metropolitan areas. The number of Indians living on reservations has been decreasing in recent years, partly because of government policies that encouraged Indian families to move to urban areas. Forty-three percent of American Indians now live in urban areas, although the majority of elderly Indians remain on reservations. Exactly what percentage of all ethnic groups is represented in the large migration to the suburbs that has occurred since 1945 is an important research question.

All of these ethnic groups have been able to attain some social mobility in the United States, although unfortunately not at the same rate. As Markson (1979) has commented, ethnic older persons have not shared in the recent success of the younger generations, who have benefited from better education and increased white-collar job opportunities. In fact, some researchers have contended that ethnic aged people, especially those from nonwhite groups, suffer from double jeopardy: they are both old, a devalued status in American society, and members of minority groups that have always suffered from discrimination (Jackson 1970). The validity of this argument and the general similarities and differences in status among aged members of ethnic groups remain to be determined (Dowd and Bengtson 1978).

Format of the Book

The question of resources and needs of ethnic aged people will be one of this volume's major focuses. Before arriving at that point, we need to be able to place this group within the framework of the field of ethnicity. Chapter 1 will examine the concept of ethnicity and the various models of ethnicity that social scientists have proposed. Having arrived at a working definition of ethnicity, we can then proceed in Chapter 2 to an examination of ethnic aged persons, with an emphasis on their sociocultural characteristics. This chapter will attempt to pull together current knowledge in the study of ethnicity and aging and will include an examination of the role of ethnicity in support systems for the elderly. The role of ethnicity in health, mental health, and social services for aged citizens will be the topic of Chapter 3. The book will conclude with a summation in Chapter 4 that attempts to provide a direction for future efforts in the area of ethnicity and aging, focusing on changes that may have an impact on ethnic groups in American society and on upcoming generations of ethnic aged.

References

Dowd, J. and Bengtson, V. 1978. Aging in minority populations: An examination of the double jeopardy hypothesis. *Journal of Gerontology* 33: 427–436.

Jackson, J. 1970. Aged Negroes: Their cultural departures from statistical stereotypes and rural-urban differences. *Gerontologist* 10: 140–145.

Markson, E. 1979. Ethnicity as a factor in the institutionalization of the ethnic elderly. In D. Gelfand and A. Kutzik (eds.), *Ethnicity and aging: Theory, research and policy*. New York: Springer.

Torres-Gil, F. and Negm, M. 1980. Policy issues concerning the Hispanic elderly. *Aging,* Nos. 305 306, 2–5.

Urban Resources Consultants. 1978. *Issue paper on the minority aging.* Washington, D.C.

Wallechinsky, D. and Wallace, I. 1978. *The people's almanac.* New York: Bantam.

Weed, P. 1973. *The white ethnic movement and ethnic politics.* New York: Praeger.

Williams, B. *Characteristics of the black elderly.* 1980. Washington, D.C.: Administration on Aging.

Chapter

1

The
Development
of Ethnic
Groups

One of the ongoing debates in social science revolves around the relationship between class and ethnicity. If ethnicity is a vital element in the lives of many different groups, then its influence should be evident among groups from many socioeconomic backgrounds. Thus the behavior and attitudes of upper-class as well as lower-class individuals should bear evidence of the importance of ethnic culture. On the other side of this argument are theorists who argue that ethnicity is only important among new immigrants to a country or groups who are forced to remain in subordinate positions. Jacquelyne Jackson, who was instrumental in focusing increased attention on elderly blacks during the 1970s, has argued that "when appropriate socioeconomic controls are used, race seems to become irrelevant as a determinant of retirement conditions, attitudes and activities" (1980, p. 10). If Jackson is correct, as groups such as blacks achieve greater social mobility, they will abandon traits distinctly related to their ethnic backgrounds in favor of attitudes and behaviors that are part of the dominant culture. In fact, it has been argued that abandonment of an ethnic culture may be a prerequisite for attaining social mobility in many societies.

A compromise between exclusive reliance on class and on ethnicity as an explanatory variable is the thesis that these two sets of variables cannot be separated. Lower-class Italians may have developed a distinctive life-style that contrasts with that of middle-class Jews. Such life-styles may stem from a melding of class and ethnic variables in a way that affords these groups the option of maintaining important elements of their ethnic culture while adopting attitudes and behaviors consonant with their social class.

It is doubtful that a resolution of the controversy over the relative importance of class and ethnicity will occur in the near future, partly because of the lack of longitudinal and cross-sectional research that adequately controls for these two variables. In terms of particular age cohorts, it would be impossible to deal with the issue of class versus ethnicity without understanding the theoretical underpinnings of ethnicity and the historical roots of the present cohort of ethnic aged people in the United States. This chapter will review the conceptions of ethnicity now current in social science and then turn to a brief detailing of the history of ethnic groups in the United States. Given the short history of the nation, it is not surprising that many ethnic aged are either members of immigrant groups or children of immigrants. Understanding the immigration patterns of both whites and nonwhites and the turmoil that has constantly buffeted native Americans is vital for understanding the impact of both class and ethnicity on aged people.

Conceptions of Ethnicity

Ethnic groups exist in many societies. A crucial aspect of these groups is that they are subunits of the majority society in which they are living. While there is disagreement over whether the Polish population in Poland constitutes an ethnic group (Greeley 1972; Kolm 1977), Poles in the United States are clearly an ethnic group. As subunits of the society, such groups are created either by their migration to another society or by the in-migration of a larger group from outisde their country. The development of ethnic groups within a country can differ drastically according to whether such subunits migrated into the country or were native groups that became dominated by other cultures that entered at a later period (Lieberson 1961).

In Malaysia, for example, native Malays have had a difficult time adjusting to the aggressive entrepreneurial interests of Chinese immigrants. In contrast, many of the groups that entered Australia during the early 1900s have occupied a subordinate position to the Australians of English descent who were the original settlers of this colony. A similar position has been held by Poles, Italians, Eastern European Jews, and other white ethnics who entered the United States during the latter part of the nineteenth and early part of the twentieth centuries. All of these groups entered this country with unique customs and beliefs and were forced to accommodate to at least some of the life-styles and demands of the English-dominated society. Minority groups such as blacks, who entered the country in servitude or to carry out jobs unwanted by others, have had to fight desperately to loosen the control maintained by dominant white groups.

Aside from differences in their initial historical experience of migration, ethnic groups have often differed in status within their countries of origin. This status has affected the education, jobs, and financial resources they attained in the "old country." In general it is fair to say that the resources which most of the European and non-European groups have possessed when they came to deal with American society were limited and these men and women represented an unskilled labor pool. Groups that were among the earlier immigrants have thus had greater amounts of time to better their position, and until recently this was reflected in available data on socioeconomic differentials among ethnic groups and among ethnic older persons.

Even immigrants with skills may not be able to find immediate employment in a new country because of language problems, a lack of jobs, or licensing requirements. This situation has been true of some of the Russian Jews who entered the United States during the 1970s. Over a period of time these obstacles may be overcome. The immigrant in his or her fifties may view these obstacles as too forbidding and thus never achieve the status he or she had in the country of origin.

Defining Ethnicity

As should already be clear, we are using *ethnicity* in this volume to designate a variety of groups that have a distinctive sense of peoplehood. This sense may be based on race, religion, or national identity (Gordon 1964). To this basic definition Shibutani and Kwan add an important element of perception: ". . . an ethnic group consists of those who conceive of themselves as being alike by virtue of their common ancestry, real or fictitious, or are so regarded by others" (1965, p. 47).

Although they focus on the characteristics of minority groups, the efforts of Wagley and Harris (1958) are applicable to many ethnic groups. Minority groups are subunits of the society with distinct physical and cultural characteristics, and strong ties exist between the members because of these characteristics. Members of these groups transmit their heritage, marry endogamously (within the group), and maintain a life-style distinct from that of the majority society.

While we may generalize these patterns to many ethnic groups, the term *minority* has also been used loosely to denote nonethnic populations such as women, the poor, and ex-convicts. As

Kolm (1977) notes, "the main focus of ethnic groups is on cultural continuity, while the focus of minority groups is mainly on equality regarding economic benefits, civil rights, political rights, etc." (p. 25). Minority groups usually attempt to create change, while ethnic groups may emphasize stability so as to maintain their value systems.

Ethnicity and Assimilation

American social scientists have been intrigued by ethnicity, but are hard pressed to formulate models of change among ethnic groups that satisfactorily match the American experience. One of the earliest and most influential formulations was that of Robert Park (1950), who proposed a "race relations cycle." For Park, the basic principles of plant and animal ecology were applicable to social life. Competition and conflict between groups appeared natural, as did the resulting accommodation of each group to the needs and demands of the other. The final stage in the Park cycle was the assimilation of one group into the other.

Park's cycle fit the evolutionary models that were popular in the 1920s. However, the failure of ethnic groups to be completely absorbed into American society proved troublesome to Park's theory, and he attributed these failures to "natural obstacles." His attempt to define these obstacles never proved wholly satisfactory, and the cycle fell into relative disuse. However, it was important as one of the major formulations of a belief that came to be more popularly known as the melting-pot approach.

This term was taken from a poem written by Israel Zangwill in 1909. To Zangwill, the "melting" of all ethnic cultures into something "American" would be of great benefit to the society. Zangwill thus differed from those who derided the un-American cultures which were still being maintained in ethnic enclaves within major American cities. He recognized that ethnic cultures would make an important contribution to the development of the ultimate American, whom he assumed would reflect a blending of all cultures rather than from adoption of an Anglo culture.

Failure of the Melting Pot

Night school and the introduction of curricula on American values and citizenship failed fully to wash away the ethnic characteristics of most immigrants. Some identifying marks did disappear as immigrants began to adopt American clothing styles and food, but many of their important attitudes and behaviors remained rooted in the Old Country.

By the late 1930s and 1940s it was clear that the melting pot was more a wish than a reality. Philosophers such as Horace Kallen (1924) had earlier called on Americans to respect the uniqueness of ethnic culture and accept a "pluralistic society" in which a variety of cultures coexisted as equals. Pluralism was not acceptable to many Americans. Nothing but a shift in values, abandonment of any foreign language, and a wholesale assimilation into a supposedly American culture would be sufficient to these critics of pluralism. The desire and difficulty of fusing a diverse polyglot of peoples coming into the United States into one new national identity as American was one factor in growing sentiment for closing off of immigration during the early 1900s. But even if pluralism had been a more acceptable model, ethnic cultures would not have stayed completely uninfluenced by industrial and urban America.

As increased contacts among ethnic groups began to take place at work, if not in the more segregated residential communities, the pace of intermarriages appeared to increase. In 1944 Ruby Jo Kennedy developed statistical analyses that indicated that such marriages were occurring along religious lines. Irish Catholics were marrying Catholics of other nationalities, and Protestants were intermarrying with Protestants of other nationalities, but Jews and blacks were maintaining their strongly endogamous patterns.

Kennedy's analysis was expanded upon by Will Herberg, who argued in the 1950s that American society was moving toward a "triple melting pot": the tripartite division of Jews, Protestants, and Catholics. Herberg's (1955) hypothesis seemed to be supported by the increasing church membership in the 1950s. This apparent religious revival coincided with the growth of the suburbs. The triple-melting-pot thesis did not maintain credence beyond the 1950s, when the expected religious revival failed to materialize and ethnic communities based on old nationality patterns continued to be maintained in many major cities.

Acculturation and Assimilation

A less sweeping model that allows us to view the current place of ethnic groups on some scale of assimilation has been developed by Milton Gordon (1964). In Gordon's model, ethnic groups may move through a number of steps toward assimilation, although they do not necessarily pass through every stage. They may skip some stages entirely. In the final assimilation stage the group abandons any identification with its ethnic background. Instead of maintaining an ethnically based culture, it accepts what Gordon has termed Anglo-conformity. Anglo-conformity assumes the "desirability of maintaining in English institutions . . . the English language, and English-oriented cultural patterns as dominant and standard in American life" (Gordon 1961, p. 264).

The first stage on the path to Anglo-conformity is behavioral assimilation, or "acculturation," the process by which immigrant groups adapt to the host society. This adaptation enables the immigrants to survive physically and economically in their new environment. The next stage, "structural assimilation," is the most crucial and occurs after the ethnic-group members have successfully achieved acculturation in the majority society. With this success, it may now be possible for ethnic-group members to intermingle with individuals from other ethnic backgrounds, including those whose social status is considerably higher. Intermingling in voluntary organizations, clubs, and cliques increases the chances that the next stage, of intermarriage or "amalgamation," will occur.

Racially based intermarriage or miscegenation has been feared by southern whites who have recognized the importance of structural assimilation. Their resistance to school integration and integration of private clubs indicates an understanding of the effects of primary association between racial and ethnic groups. Gordon cautions that structural assimilation is not a prerequisite for greater blending of ethnic groups, but that once it occurs, the likelihood of intermarriage increases. Groups such as Jews who have been concerned about the stability of their culture and values have also recognized this fact, attempting to place strong taboos on intermarriage. We can locate major ethnic groups at different positions on this model, which indicates more clearly than other models the complexity of cultural change among such groups.

Groups that are allowed to enter the primary cliques and intermarry within a society are also likely to develop a sense of identity with the dominant group, possible abandoning their prior identification as Poles, Japanese, Jews, or whatever. This stage of assimilation Gordon denotes as "identificational."

Groups that come to be valued and accepted by the dominant society will reach a point where they experience no prejudice or discrimination toward them. In turn they may alter their belief systems so that they eliminate issues of value and power that previously differentiated them from majority groups. These three latter stages, called "attitudinal receptional," "behavior receptional," and "civic assimilational," may not occur even though an individual ethnic group has progressed through all of the other stages and has abandoned any individual sense of peoplehood (Gordon 1964). While ethnic groups with high rates of intermarriage closely approximate the assimilationist position, others still maintain high rates of endogamy and a continued emphasis on important elements of the traditional culture. A third pattern adopted by ethnic groups may be to abandon some distinctive attitudes and behaviors but maintain those elements that group members believe are crucial to their survival as a distinct cultural entity.

Whether an individual or an ethnic group moves through some or all of these stages is important to the elderly. Intermarriage may mean that children do not show a strong interest in ethnic customs and celebrations. In many ethnic cultures the older person plays an honored and respected role in the family and the community. Full assimilation may mean that traditional patterns of respect and honor for older persons, as well as traditional expectations of assistance for them, fall by the wayside, unless these traditions are an important element in the internalized value system of the individual.

In Chapter 4 we will return to Gordon's model to assess the current and possible future status of major ethnic groups and the position of the aged within these groups.

Ethnicity and Identity

The issue of ethnic survival raises the equally complex issue of identity. If ethnicity is a salient variable in personal identity, then we should expect it to survive in some form whatever the role of intermarriage among groups. Some of Horace Kallen's most impassioned writings embrace the idea of ethnicity as an integral part of identity.

Dashefsky (1976) has attempted to provide a conceptualization of identity that we can apply to ethnicity. An individual's identity can be defined by that individual or by others. However, alternative criteria form the basis for these definitions. If an individual's identity is defined by others (social identity), it may be based on a number of broad categorical attributes, including occupation, age, or ethnicity. Personal identity is based not on these broad scale attributes, but rather on elements that are unique to a specific individual. These may include relationships of the individual with other family members or general personality traits.

Again, when the individual attempts to define himself or herself, he or she may base the choice of characteristics on large-scale structural attributes or on individualized components. A set of attitudes held by the individual based on ethnic-group membership, occupation, or age may form the core of the individual's self-conception. On the other hand, deep-seated, less conscious ideas of the individual (ego-identity) may not be so apparent unless they are brought to the surface through intense probing. It is possible that here also ethnic background may prove crucial.

Ethnic identification can be important for the individual at a number of levels. The person may be seen as "ethnic" by other members of the society even though he or she expresses little interest in the ethnic culture. This ethnic identification can be based on visible elements such as physical characteristics or manner of dress. As acculturation and intermarriages increase, ease of identification based on these measures becomes more difficult, and people must rely increasingly on unreliable indicators such as surnames.

Groups concerned about maintaining segregation and quotas must utilize a number of measures. In the past, photos on application forms for college and employment enabled organizations to discriminate against nonwhites. Personal interviews for employment accomplished the same task. In toto, however, the decreased visibility of many ethnic characteristics may account for the tendency of some researchers and practitioners to ignore the ethnic background of their white clients. This is in sharp contrast to a variable such as age, which remains a visible and identifiable characteristic of personal identity. Such visible attributes may provide convenient and economical ways in which to classify individuals, since personal details related to identity are known only to a small circle of intimates.

Many individuals may now be making conscious decisions about whether to utilize their ethnic background as a basis for their own self-conception. According to a common view of ethnic history in the United States, first-generation immigrants in the past attempted to acculturate in order to survive in the new society while still holding on to the cultural roots which provided a sense of identity and security. The second generation did not face the same difficulties in coping with their environment. Their English was fluent and their knowledge of the business and bureaucratic worlds more complete. To these second-generation Americans the ethnic heritage was not necessarily a refuge, but rather an embarrassing reminder of a period when their parents slaved in sweatshops in order to survive and were preyed upon by a wide variety of merchants, employers, and politicians. Many second-generation individuals moved away from the ethnic community both geographically and spiritually. Changing an ethnic name into a more Anglo-Saxon equivalent was often a culminating step in this process. A "return" to the ethnic culture was a choice for the third generation. Having economic and psychological security, these grandchildren of the original migrants could decide either to ignore the ethnic culture or to adopt some of its more interesting and colorful and less restricting elements.

This model of intergenerational change must be seen as an "ideal" type, since decisions of the second or third generation about the role of ethnicity in all aspects of their lives have never been clear-cut. Althcugh second-generation members of ethnic groups might move away from an involvement in ethnic culture, they may carry on a tradition of respect and assistance for older persons. Such traditions may be strongly internalized and resist the changes that occur among each succeeding generation.

The adoption of many elements of the traditional ethnic culture by the third generation is viewed by sociologists and psychologists as an attempt by individuals to find tangible ways to express their identity in the face of a relatively impersonal society in which life-styles and occupations are homogenized. The relationship of this interest in ethnicity to ego identity as defined by Dashefsky (1976) is as yet undetermined. It is also not yet clear whether this is a return to a gastric culture in which bagels, pizza, and moussaka are unthreatening symbols of ethnicity, or a reawakening of a deeper interest in the ethnic heritage.

While the third generation may find it easy to return to ethnicity as an important base for personal identity, the history of ethnic populations in American society indicates that each ethnic group has fought vigorously to preserve its identity in the face of intense hostility from the Anglo-dominated society. First- and second-generation individuals who carried on this battle now comprise the dominant segment of the ethnic aged population.

The struggle for ethnic survival has been true of groups distinguishable on the basis of national origin, race, or religion. Blacks arrived on American shores as slaves, Irish were branded as drunken illiterates, and Mormons were seen as threatening enough for the Illinois militia to engage in battle with them in 1838 (McMurray & Cunningham 1973). Another major thrust of American antipathy towards ethnic groups has been directed against Catholics (Higham 1972). The experience of practically all ethnic groups in the United States has been one of turmoil and at least initial hardships. To understand the present position, attitudes, and behavior of the ethnic aged we need to turn our attention to a brief examination of the ethnic immigrants to the United States.

The History of Immigration

The first immigrants were blacks who came involuntarily to the United States in the 1600s, and to Latin America even earlier. Ironically, slave traders in Latin America did not originally intend to use blacks as slaves, but instead attempted to subjugate native Indians. This was unsuccessful, as Indians in Brazil escaped to the impenetrable jungles or proved easy victims of the diseases that the white settlers brought from Europe (Harris 1964).

The second wave of immigration to the United States was from the northern parts of Europe. Economics based on failing single-crop agricultures, repressive taxation, and persecution of religious groups prompted this wave of emigration. The "old" immigration of the 1830s was followed by the "new" immigration from southern and eastern Europe in the late 1800s and early 1900s, which brought groups such as Italians, Poles, and Russian Jews in great numbers to this country.

Immigration and Industrialization

The earliest nineteenth-century immigrants to the United States found a society that was beginning to embark full tilt on an aggressive course of industrialization. Historians have emphasized the period after the Civil War in discussing the growth of the urban, industrial United States, but this process had begun by the middle of the 1830s. It should have been clear to most contemporary observers that the agricultural society of the eighteenth century was going to be replaced by an industrial economy. Although Alexis de Tocqueville failed to be as far-sighted about this change as he was about other attributes of American society, he did warn in his classic *Democracy in America* (1840) of the danger that an "aristocracy of manufacturers" would develop in this country.

Changes in work patterns produced by the new emphasis on large-scale manufacturing quickly became evident. Warner (1973) has noted that in Philadelphia in 1844, working relations based on the relaxed pace of the small shop were already giving way to the more rigid schedule of the factory. Increased immigration and competition for the new jobs swelled incipient antagonisms among ethnic groups. The history of interethnic relations in Philadelphia clearly points to this problem (Warner 1973). In 1835 Philadelphia welcomed 1890 immigrants. Five years later, 4079 immigrants arrived in the city. Unfortunately, these immigrants arrived at a time of severe economic depression, which lasted from 1837 to 1843. One of the results of the depression was antiblack and anti-Irish riots in the city, since these two groups bore the brunt of the blame for the current economic miseries.

The Irish were not the only immigrants to encounter hostility. As people from southern and eastern Europe began to arrive in the United States during the last part of the nineteenth century, the earlier Irish and German immigrants began to appear in a better light to writers of the period. As Stoddard wrote in 1920:

> The white race divides into three main sub-species—the Nordics, the Alpines and the Mediterraneans. All three are good

stocks, ranking in genetic worth well above the various colored races. However, there seems to be no question that the Nordic is far and away the most valuable type. . . . Our country, originally settled almost exclusively by Nordics, was towards the close of the nineteenth century invaded by hordes of immigrant Alpines and Mediterraneans, not to mention Asiatic elements like Levantines and Jews. As a result, the Nordic native American has been crowded out with amazing rapidity by the swarming prolific aliens. (Stoddard 1920, cited in Simpson and Yinger 1965, p. 90)

Of course, the negative comparison of the immigrants of the 1890s with earlier immigrants was only a restatement of the negative comments of the 1830s, which compared the lack of quality of immigrants of that period with the worth of even earlier arrivals.

While the new ethnic groups appeared to be different from earlier groups, each succeeding wave of immigration helped to feed the industrial machine that began to pound out products more rapidly after the Civil War. In many plants, the manufacturers were distressed by the seemingly sloppy work habits of their employees, who often needed Mondays off to recover from their weekend binges. Many immigrants tolerated poor working and living conditions because they had no intention of staying in the United States. Between 1908 and 1910, forty-four eastern and southern Europeans returned to Europe for every hundred that arrived (Gutman 1976).

As immigration showed no signs of abating in the early 1900s, a more widespread negative reaction began to take hold among the American public. Fears of epidemics spread by the poor living conditions of immigrants in the cities became prevalent. Another fear was that bolshevism, which was beginning to make headway in eastern Europe, would be fomented in the United States by the new immigrants (Williams 1966).

Closing of Immigration

By 1921 all of the tensions of racism, unionization, and radicalism had combined to cause the closing of immigration with the passage of the Quota Act. This act allowed people to emigrate to the United States in proportion to their country's representation in the American population of 1910. With its passage, immigration from overseas dropped from 500,000 individuals a year to around 150,000. The use of 1910 as the base year for determining quotas naturally meant that larger quotas went to North European countries. Great Britain alone was allotted 40 percent of the annual quota of immigrants; including Ireland and Germany accounted for almost 70 percent of the total. In 1924 the Johnson-Reed Act established 1890 as the census year on which quotas were to be based. Since there were less "new" immigrants in the United States in that year, the quota for southern and eastern Europeans under this act was even less than it had been using the 1910 base year (Mann 1979). Asians were basically excluded from immigration into the country under the new law.

There were changes in this law. The Brides Act of 1945 allowed spouses, children, or fiancées of members of the armed forces to immigrate and the Displaced Persons Act of 1948 permitted refugees from World War II to enter the United States, but the McCarran-Walter Act of 1952 reaffirmed the quota system. Many immigrants thus entered the country under special legislation such as was passed after the uprising in Hungary in 1956.

In 1965 the quota system was finally abolished. Beginning in 1968 the Immigration Act repealed discrimination against Asians and allowed 170,000 immigrants from the eastern hemisphere and 120,000 immigrants from the western hemisphere entrance to the U.S. on a first-come, first-qualified basis. These qualifications related to the seven preference categories set up under the legislation. Four preferences were for family reunion, two for professional and unskilled workers needed in this country, and one preference was for refugees. Parents and spouses of U.S. citizens are exempt from the act's limitations.

In the 1970s the immigration picture began to change dramatically, with individuals entering the United States as either immigrants or refugees. In 1980 approximately 300,000 immigrants entered the United States under regular immigration provisions. In addition to these individuals a large number of refugees arrived from Indochina. In November 1980 there were 435,000 Indochinese refugees living in the United States with the largest group (142,000) in California (Refugee Report, 1981).

In order to develop some standard policy concerning refugees, the Refugee Act of 1980 was passed by the ninety-sixth Congress. Under this act a flow of 50,000 refugees is allowed into the United States on an annual basis until fiscal 1983. This number could be exceeded if the President after consultation with the House of Representatives and Senate Judiciary Committees decided that an expanded number was warranted by humanitarian concerns. Beginning in 1983 the President must annually set the allocation of refugees after consultation with Congress. A refugee is defined by the act as an individual who is outside his country and is persecuted or fears persecution upon return to his country.

Over 100,000 Cubans and Haitians migrated to the United States in 1980 but these new residents were not classified as refugees because of the definition's emphasis on individuals fleeing from political persecution. In 1981 three to six million illegal aliens were also living in this country, some intending to stay in the United

States for only a short period of time in order to earn sufficient money to return home and support their families. Many of these aliens have come from Mexico and the Dominican Republic. Their presence as illegal workers on farms and in factories has created tensions in many communities and in American relations with a number of Latin American countries.

In 1981 the Select Commission on Immigration and Refugee Policy appointed by President Carter completed a two year study of immigration and submitted its final report. Among the Commission's recommendations are amnesty for all illegal aliens who were in the United States as of January 1, 1980, an increased budget for the Border Patrol to help control immigration and the imposition of penalties for employers who hire illegal aliens.

The Commission also recommended that the total immigration quota be raised to 350,000 with an additional 100,000 individuals being admitted during the next five years to clear up the backlog of applications from would-be immigrants. If these recommendations were adopted it is estimated that the United States would have to absorb between 650,000–800,000 immigrants annually. These recommendations will certainly spark renewed debate about the role of the United States as a haven from repression, a land of economic opportunity, and a pluralistic society.

Although the development of an optimal immigration policy remains a thorny issue, the closing of immigration in the 1920s means that the present generation of older white ethnics (over 75) arrived during the heyday of immigration. They lived, at least during the early years, in another country. The younger group of elderly whites and the upcoming generation of older white adults are more likely to have been born in this country and to have been exposed to the culture of the old country only as it was transmitted by their parents or experienced travelers. Maintenance of ethnic culture among the next few generations of white ethnic aged in the United States will not be assisted by large numbers of incoming Europeans. It will instead have to be transmitted through the explicit and implicit behavior and attitudes of individuals already residing in the United States.

Immigrants and Minorities in the U.S.

Each of the white and nonwhite groups that now comprise a part of American society has had to develop means of dealing with the problems of adaptation that are consonant with their own culture. In order to highlight some of the major events that have affected these diverse groups, we can first examine the conditions and opportunities these immigrants encountered upon arrival in the

United States during the 1890s, a period when European immigration was at its height. Second, we can select three major ethnic groups as examples of the acculturation process required for survival in this country: Jews, a religioethnic group which emigrated to the United States to escape persecution and to obtain economic and social advancement; Japanese, a nonwhite group that arrived for both cultural and economic reasons; and finally, American Indians, who were the original settlers of the country but still had to meet the demands of white settlers who insisted on drastic alterations in their culture and style of life.

America in the 1890s

By the 1890s the United States had firmly embarked on its program of industrialization within a capitalistic economy. In 1890 the Census Bureau declared that the frontier was closed and that there were no new lands for Americans to conquer on the continent. Growth was now going to be in the cities. In fact, by 1890 all of the major American cities except for Los Angeles were already in existence. A symbol of this growth was Frederick Jackson Turner's famous 1893 paper in which he predicted negative consequences from the closing of the frontier (Turner 1920).

It should not be surprising that many immigrants saw the cities as offering needed opportunities. Coming from European agricultural communities, groups such as Italians associated farming with the poverty they were trying so hard to escape. Instead of attempting to farm again, they turned to construction. In New York in 1905, the largest percentage of Italians (45 percent) were working as unskilled laborers. Forty percent of the Jewish males in New York in the same year were employed in the clothing industry (Gutman 1976). In the case of Poles, new opportunities seemed to be associated with the heavy industries opening up in Cleveland, Chicago, and Buffalo.

In the cities the immigrants moved into areas peopled by individuals from their own ethnic background. Immigrant aid societies helped the newcomers adjust to their environment. While emigration from the Old Country produced strains on the family, European immigrants managed to sustain their family structures. Gutman's (1976) data indicate that in both the industrial city of Paterson, New Jersey, and New York, the percentage of immigrants with intact families was extremely high. In 1880 in Paterson the percentage of nuclear households among British, German, Irish, and native whites was 74, 78, 73, and 65, respectively. The nuclear family also remained an important element of the ethnic culture of Jews and Italians. Ninety-six percent of the Jews and 95 percent of the Italians in New York during 1905 lived within a nuclear household. A large percentage of "augmented" families—that is, families that included lodgers—also appeared among both Jews and Italians. Some of the lodgers were single men or men who arrived in the United States first and planned to bring their families over as soon as they had earned the passage money.

Jewish Americans

The Jews who settled on the Lower East Side of New York were able to reestablish much of their traditional communal life. It would be a mistake, however, to assume that the ethnic communities in which today's elderly were raised were ever totally isolated from the larger environment. Some Jewish religious leaders let out anguished cries about the temptations that led many Jews away from orthodoxy. The film *Hester Street,* for instance, portrays the pressures placed on new Jewish immigrants to conform to at least the more obvious elements of American culture, including dress and language. However, local stores provided the Jews with the kosher foods they needed, and the new settlement houses which provided social services were staffed by Jews oriented to the culture and needs of their immigrant clients.

While the orientation of shops and agencies to the needs of the community sounds comforting, we should not underestimate the poverty and hostility that the immigrants encountered. Their high disease rates and short life expectancies can be attributed in part to the poor environmental conditions under which they lived.

The writings of muckrakers such as Lincoln Steffens and Jacob Riis were important in bringing these substandard living conditions to the attention of the public. Though the work of these reformers was laudable, many of them had strong beliefs about the genetic nature of the qualities they noticed among immigrants. Riis (1970) commented on the counting ability and the secretiveness of the Jews. Blacks, of course, he assumed to be racially inferior. Despite these stereotypic and mistaken beliefs, however, the early reformers worked valiantly to improve living conditions. The social reforms they helped promote have had more impact on the children of the immigrants than on the immigrants themselves, who have entered their old age with limited education, limited fluency in English, and minimal incomes.

Japanese-Americans

As has been true of blacks, Japanese and Chinese have always proved vulnerable targets for whites attempting to divert attention from troublesome issues. The scapegoat role that blacks have played in the North and South has been occupied by Orientals on the West Coast. Hostility toward the Japanese was used by some politicians to win elections. A relatively weak political group, the Japanese were unable to fend off these unwarranted attacks.

Some people always complained that the Japanese did not "fit in." One reason they did not fit into American society was their racial distinctiveness. As Woodrow Wilson remarked when campaigning for election as President in 1912, "The whole question is one of assimilation of diverse races. We cannot make a homogeneous population of a people who do not blend with the Caucasian race" (cited in Simpson and Yinger 1965, p. 92).

A second reason that the Japanese did not fit in was their seeming failure even to want to adapt to the American way of life. Modell (1968) has provided a fascinating historical approach to this issue which furnishes an understanding of the attitudes and behaviors of the Issei—the first generation of Japanese immigrants. As Modell notes, the Issei were not a particularly successful group in Japan. Over two-thirds of them had been working in agriculture. They were drawn to the United States by factors that went beyond simple economic survival; immigration "stood as an expedient for preserving what appeared to them to be the substance of Japanese family organization which overpopulation had rendered precarious in Japan" (Modell 1968, p. 73). To preserve the family effectively required the Issei to remain distinct and separate from an American culture that was divergent in basic orientation from their own.

Unfortunately, total isolation is not possible for a cultural group living within a larger culture, even if they maintain strong, ethnically homogeneous residential communities. Despite external influences, however, the effort to maintain Issei culture resulted in a distinctive pattern of Japanese acculturation to American society. The Issei learned enough English to survive but continued to rely on families for assistance, a pattern that was possible since many of the group's members lived within extended kin networks. Many of the Issei also maintained contact with Japan.

The reluctance of the Japanese to integrate socially with other groups left them relatively defenseless as pressures for their exclusion from the United States mounted. In 1905 the California legislature passed a resolution urging Congress to exclude Japanese from the United States; in 1906 San Francisco schools barred Japanese children; and in 1907 the American government negotiated a famous agreement with the Japanese government, the terms of which limited the number of passports it issued for emigration to the United States. In 1924, when the Quota Act was passed, no Asian group was allotted a quota.

In the aftermath of the bombing of Pearl Harbor in 1941,

stereotyping and racial antagonism toward the Japanese again came to the forefront. Hostility on the part of large landowners toward the increasingly successful Japanese farmers also contributed to the order that placed the Japanese in "relocation camps" for the duration of the war. As one Nisei noted, Japanese-Americans expected that the Issei who were not American citizens were going to be evacuated, but the thought never occurred to them that the Nisei, the second-generation American-born children, would also be relocated.

The years of internment were extremely damaging to Japanese-Americans. While they have slowly received monetary restitution for the loss of their lands, Japanese-American farmers have been forced to move into new occupations, most notably gardening on the West Coast and large corporation work in cities such as Chicago.

The forced communal environment of the relocation camps had an extensive effect on the traditional Japanese family structure. In these camps decision making on the part of committees quickly began to replace decisions made by parents and carried out without questioning by children. For many Issei, participation in decision making by committees was not possible, since it contradicted traditional family roles. The Issei were also at a disadvantage because leadership in the relocation camps fell on the shoulders of individuals who could successfully negotiate with the civilian authorities. This required an understanding of the American political process and a fluency in English that were not common among the Issei. The years in the camps were thus important in the weakening of traditional family roles, which allowed the Nisei to emerge as an important element in the Japanese-American community earlier than would otherwise have been possible.

American Indians

Both Japanese and Jews were immigrants who came to the United States seeking some important goal fulfillment. Differences in traditions and race accounted in some measure for the nature of their varied historical encounters with the Anglo-dominated American culture. Yet the group that has suffered most from its dealings with the dominant American culture is the one group that was not immigrant but native to the continent.

Despite popular impressions, the injustices and murders perpetrated on American Indians have failed to destroy the tribes. In fact, the Indian territories appear to be growing. At present the lands included in Indian reservations comprise some 90 million acres. This acreage is expanding as some tribal groups, such as those in Maine, aggressively press their legal claims to state land.

Although we can discuss native Americans as a group, it is important to note that Indian groups are extremely diverse, with important tribal differences. A primary characteristic of Indian tribes, though, has been their dependence on oral tradition, in which the elderly pass down culture and history to younger generations in words rather than by written documentation.

Native Americans found that whites were not prepared to leave such traditions intact, but instead were implacable in their demands that Indians acculturate or be destroyed. For example, the demand that Indians settle in one area was contrary to the living patterns of some tribes. A nomadic pattern of life could not easily fit into a dominant culture that placed great emphasis on the concept of ownership of land and the inalienable right of the owner to use property in any way he or she wished. Even more settled tribes believed that land was communal property. The concept that individuals own land and then pass it on to their children has never been accepted by many tribes.

In 1887 the Dawes Severalty Act disbanded the tribes as legal entities entitled to hold land. Acreage on the reservations was distributed among families who were to become owners in twenty-five years. Many Indians who were unused to intensive farming were unable to survive off their property and sold it to whites before the twenty-five years had passed. These Indians then became paupers dependent on government assistance. The Dawes Act was finally repealed in 1934. Its replacement was the Indian Reorganization Act, which aimed to make the reservations more self-sufficient in terms of resources, education, and business opportunities. In the 1950s the federal approach again shifted, in an attempt to terminate the relationship between the government and the tribes by encouraging the Indians to move off the reservations and into the urban society. Some Indians who left for the cities were able to obtain jobs as steelworkers or high girder workers. Others, finding the urban culture totally alien, began to experience emotional difficulties.

Despite the government's inability to maintain a historically consistent policy stance toward native Americans, the attitudes of non-Indian administrators on the reservation has usually been to enforce an assimilationist stance. As McGregor describes the process in the past:

> Children were virtually kidnaped to force them into government schools, their hair was cut, and their Indian clothes were thrown away. They were forbidden to speak in their own language. Life in the school was under military discipline, and rules were enforced by corporal punishment. Those who persisted in clinging

to their old ways and those who ran away and were recaptured were thrown into jail. Parents who objected were also jailed. Where possible, children were kept in school year after year to avoid the influence of their families. (MacGregor, cited in Simpson and Yinger 1965, p. 145)

The history of native Americans has been characterized by vaccillation on the part of the American government. From a period in which genocide seemed to be the order of the day, the government has moved through various programs, each designed to promote the final assimilation of the Indian. In turn, Indian leaders have branded each of these programs as a subtle form of genocide. The ideal of a pluralistic society has never included the Indians as one of its constituent groups. If the 1970s and 1980s are the beginning of a real change on the part of American society toward the Indian, then we may see the development of an assertive Indian culture that comes to grips with how much acculturation is necessary for success in terms of its belief system.

The Uniqueness of American Attitudes

While the history of the treatment of native Americans may seem particularly brutal, there can be no question that all of the minority and ethnic groups that are now considered part of American society have faced major difficulties in adapting to an Anglo-dominated culture which demands major changes in behavior and values. That this has happened is not unique. The ethnic conflicts that have taken place around the world are legion. Conflict continues among the French-Canadians, who are now reasserting their claim to independence from English-dominated Canada, and it continues in Spain, where the Basques engage in violent activities as part of a simmering separatist movement. Until the 1970s Malaysia appeared to be a bright spot in this picture, as the government tried to promote the development of a truly biracial and bicultural country, but this effort became doomed to failure when the Malays finally erupted in anti-Chinese riots. Thus, there does not seem to be anything inherent in the American personality that has led to discrimination and prejudice toward various ethnic groups. What is unique is the way in which particular ethnic groups have been singled out, the depth of the hostility toward these groups, and the responses of ethnic groups to the hostility of American society.

Elderly People and Ethnic History

If we think about the elderly in all of these ethnic groups, we should expect the history outlined in this chapter to have had an important effect on their attitudes. Indians who are now seventy-five lived through the years of the Dawes Act and the changes in American policy. Blacks of the same age may have been involved in sharecropping in the rural South or in the movement of blacks to the North at the time of early union-management conflicts. Elderly Jews struggled to attain the financial security they now possess, only to see the horrors of World War II wipe away their confidence that anti-Semitism, which had been moribund for many years, would never reawaken.

The fact that many of these older persons appear cautious in their attitudes toward change should not be unexpected. Botwinick (1978) has conducted a series of fascinating experiments in which he shows the cautiousness of older persons in choosing between alternatives. This may be viewed as very practical by a generation of people who have struggled to be able to attain a sense of security in their old age. Second- and third-generation elderly people whose history has been less troubled may be more assertive in their decision making.

Many of the first-generation elderly also struggled to maintain their ethnic culture intact. However, what they regarded as the intact culture was the culture they experienced as they grew up. For immigrants, the removal from the Old Country meant that they were unable to witness the cultural changes that took place in their native place. Instead, they froze the culture in their memories. In contrast to these memories, cultures in many of the countries of origin have altered markedly since the emigration of the now older adults.

Kitano (1969) provides interesting reports of Japanese who returned to Japan after many years of living in the United States. Japan has rapidly modernized and industrialized since World War II, experiencing some major cultural changes. For elderly Japanese, the impact of going back to this Japan which they remember so differently must be very strong.

It is thus important to realize that when we discuss the ethnic elderly, older Poles in the United States are not the same as older Poles in Poland. Poles in the United States have taken a culture, removed it from its roots, and by necessity adapted it to some degree to the demands of living in a foreign environment. The extent to which the demography and the psychological and sociological attributes of life in the country of origin remain extant among American-based ethnic elderly people is the subject of the next chapter.

References

Dashefsky, A. 1976. *Ethnic identity in society.* Chicago: Rand-McNally.
deTocqueville, A. 1961. *Democracy in America.* New York: Schocken Books (originally published 1840).

Gordon, M. 1961. Assimilation in America: Theory and reality. *Daedalus* 90(2): 263–85.

———. 1964. *Assimilation in American life*. New York: Oxford University Press.

Greeley, A. 1972. *That most distressful nation*. Chicago: Quadrangle Books.

Gutman, D. 1966. *Work, culture and society in industrializing America*. New York: Knopf.

Harris, M. 1964. *Patterns of race in the Americas*. New York: Walker and Co.

Herberg, W. 1955. *Protestant-Catholic-Jew*. New York: Doubleday.

Higham, J. 1972. *Strangers in the land: Patterns of American nativism 1860–1925*. New York: Atheneum.

Jackson, J.J. 1980. Minority elderly. *Ageing International* 7(2): 10.

Kallen, H. 1924. *Culture and democracy in the United States*. New York:Boni and Liverwright.

Kennedy, R. 1944. Single or triple melting pot? Intermarriage trends in New Haven, 1870–1940. *American Journal of Sociology* 49: 331–39.

Kitano, H. 1969. *Japanese-Americans*. Englewood Cliffs, N.J.: Prentice-Hall.

Kolm, R. 1977. *Ethnicity in social work and social work education*. Washington, D.C.: Catholic University of America.

Lieberson, S. 1961. A societal theory of race and ethnic relations. *American Sociological Review*, 26: 902-910.

Mann, A. 1979. *The one and the many: Reflections on the American identity*. Chicago: University of Chicago Press.

MacMurray, V., and Cunningham, P. 1973. Mormons and Gentiles: A study in persistence. In D. Gelfand and R. Lee (eds.), *Ethnic conflicts and power*. New York: John Wiley.

Modell, J. 1968. The Japanese American family: A perspective for future investigation. *Pacific Historical Review*, 37: 67–81.

Park, R. 1950. *Race and culture*. Glencoe, Ill.: Fress Press.

Refugee Reports. 1981. Statistical reports. 2(15): 8.

Riis, J. 1970. *How the other half lives*. Cambridge, Ma.: Harvard University Press (originally published in 1890).

Shibutani, T., and Kwan, K. 1965. *Ethnic stratification*. New York: Macmillan.

Simpson, G., and Yinger, J. 1965. *Racial and cultural minorities*. New York: Harper and Row.

Turner, F. 1920. *The frontier in American history*. New York: Macmillan.

Wagley, C., and Harris, M. 1958. *Minorities in the new world*. New York: Columbia University Press.

Warner, S. Jr. 1968. *The private city*. Philadelphia: University of Pennsylvania Press.

Williams, W. 1966. *Contours of American history*. New York: Harper.

Zangwill, I. 1909. *The melting pot*. New York: Macmillan.

Chapter

2

Ethnic
Aged
in the
United States

Describing elderly members of ethnic groups would seem to be a simple matter of compiling and presenting the appropriate statistics. As is the case with many other seemingly simple tasks, providing an accurate portrayal of the ethnic aged proves to be much more involved than we might expect.

Statistics on the socioeconomic and demographic characteristics of the ethnic aged people are difficult to compile. When we use the term "ethnic aged," we are discussing a large number of groups, including those with a base in nationality, such as Italians or Greeks; groups that have their roots in religious beliefs, such as Mormons; and ethnic groups whose sense of peoplehood has been based on the ascribed characteristics of race, such as blacks and Asians. While figures on racially based ethnic groups are now available, state and federal censuses often do not break down by nationality the figures on white groups.

Even more troublesome for our purposes is the total lack of data on the religious nature of many groups. Independent researchers collect information on the religious affiliations of their samples, and the Canadian government includes questions about religion in its census. However, the U.S. government forbids the Census Bureau to collect information about religion. As we discuss particular ethnic groups in this chapter, we will use knowledge about their dominant religious affiliation to fill in this gap in government-provided data.

Even if the available information were more complete, a recital of current figures would fail to provide an adequate understanding of the present cohort of ethnic aged people. To flesh out this understanding we must focus on a variety of other characteristics, including:

    1. the general social and cultural characteristics of ethnic aged people;

    2. the relationship between these characteristics and attitudes toward growing older;

    3. the relationship between ethnically specific characteristics and the satisfaction of ethnic aged people with their present life. During all of this discussion, we must constantly attend to the manner in which the norms of American culture have created stresses and altered the culture and life of ethnic aged people. To lay the groundwork for any further discussion, we must first turn to the data on specific characteristics of aged members of ethnic groups.

Demographic and Socioeconomic Characteristics

Immigrant and American-Born Elderly People

    In 1960 four million Americans over sixty were foreign-born. This large group primarily represents immigrants who came to the United States prior to World War I, although there was an immigration of southern and eastern Europeans after World War II. By 1970 many of the earlier immigrants had died, and the number of immigrant elderly people had declined to 3.7 million. In total this represents 14 percent of the elderly in 1970. By the end of the 1980s this group will represent only 5 percent of the older population. The passage of legislation in 1965 reduced restrictions in the immigration laws and encouraged the entry of larger numbers of Europeans into the United States. As already noted, the proportion of elderly in the recent immigrant population appears to approximate the percentage of elderly in the general American population while the proportion of elderly among refugees remains lower. The growth of Korean and Southeast Asian populations in the United States, however, will be interesting to observe, since these groups have not previously been widely represented in the ethnic mix of the United States. One final group cannot yet be accurately discussed: The three to six million illegal aliens, primarily from Central and South America, whom the Department of Immigration and Naturalization has had a difficult time controlling or even counting accurately.

    Even with gaps in figures on illegal aliens, it is clear that we are now concluding a major period of providing health and social services to older Americans born in Europe. At the end of the twentieth century and throughout the twenty-first century there will be large numbers of American born ethnic elderly and ethnic elderly from Indo-China, Asia, and Latin America.

Education and Income

The greater proportion of American-born ethnic older persons should be reflected in higher educational levels of the next cohorts of aged. The median educational level for individuals educated before the Depression of the 1930s was eight years. This contrasts with the ten to twelve years of school that represented the median educational level of whites older than sixty-five in 1978. Elderly blacks and Hispanics still lag behind in educational achievement, since their median educational level in 1978 was only five to seven years (U.S. Bureau of the Census 1978). The median educational level of older adults should continue to rise to twelve years by 1990 (Fowles 1978).

The improvement in educational levels of the elderly is also reflected to some degree in their economic situation. The median income of all elderly people has continued to rise over the past twenty years, but the median income of elderly white households in 1977 was still twice that of elderly Hispanic and black households: approximately $8000 for whites and $4000 to $5000 for Hispanics and blacks (U.S. Bureau of the Census 1978). In toto, 12 percent of elderly whites, 34 percent of the blacks, and 23 percent of the Hispanics had incomes in 1978 that were below the official government poverty threshold ($3917 for a couple and $3116 for an older individual) (U.S. Senate Special Committee on Aging 1980). Government programs such as Medicare have helped the older person keep from falling behind even further in the race to keep up with inflation.

We need to make two caveats about these seemingly positive figures on education and income of the elderly: (1) Some now contend that poverty figures as developed and used by the federal government do not reflect "hidden poverty"; and (2) minority aged have not benefited as much as white aged people from advances in education and income. Mollie Orshansky, who designed the poverty formula for the Social Security Administration in 1964, asserted in 1979 that 21 percent of the elderly were below the poverty level, rather than the 14 percent being cited by the Census Bureau in that same year (Rich 1979). To obtain her figures, Orshansky omitted from the income of aged people the income of others living in the same household. Elderly people who live with their family members, she argues, often do so because of a lack of adequate income.

At the lower end of any income measurements are those who have been immigrants and the minority aged. The immigrants occupied the lowest-paid jobs because of their inadequate education, difficulties with English, and general unfamiliarity with American culture. Minority elderly people faced discrimination that restricted their economic opportunity and even their ability to attain the education necessary for advancement and social mobility. (Thernstrom's sophisticated 1973 analysis lays to rest an alternative approach that claims that minority groups such as blacks have had retarded advancement in American society because they were the last migrants to urban centers where the highest-paying jobs are located.) Because of this retarded advancement there is a great discrepancy between white and black elderly in the availability of "unearned" income. In 1976 two-thirds of elderly white families had income from dividends, pensions, or interest, but this source of income was found only among one-sixth of all elderly black families. Black elderly are thus more likely than whites to depend on social security, earnings, and SSI (supplemental security income) for their income (Hill 1978).

The low income and educational backgrounds of elderly blacks are shared by other minority aged people. In San Diego, for example, the median educational level of elderly Chinese was 6.8 years (Cheng 1978); of elderly Latinos, 5.8 years (Valle and Mendoza 1978); of elderly Japanese, 9.8 years (Ishizuka 1978); and of elderly Filipinos, 6.9 years (Peterson 1978). With a median of 8.9 years of education, elderly blacks (Sanford 1978) were second to the Japanese, but it must be remembered that many of the European- or Asian-based groups included substantial numbers of individuals who had some difficulty speaking English or who spoke no English at all.

While ethnic elderly people have benefited from the growth in social welfare and health programs as well as income maintenance programs, their low educational levels and relegation to poor-paying positions have prevented them from obtaining the maximum benefits available from Social Security or the quality of services that higher-income elderly people expect. The gap between the living conditions of ethnic aged people and those of their more affluent age peers becomes clear when we examine specific areas such as health or housing conditions. While we cannot provide data on all ethnic aged people here, selected examples should give a good indication of the problems they face.

Health and Living Conditions of the Elderly

Elderly black males have both lower incomes and a higher prevalence of some serious illnesses than elderly white males. Recent reports indicate that the incidence of cancer is increasing among blacks, while it is declining among whites. Hypertension is also alarmingly common among elderly blacks, and indeed is more common among blacks of all ages than among whites (Jackson 1978). These and other health problems among blacks show up in employment figures, which indicate that almost 40 percent of blacks in the fifty-five to sixty-four age range were unable to work in 1969 because of health problems. The comparable figure was considerably lower among whites. Ten percent more black than white elderly people had health-related work problems (Urban Resources Consultants 1978). One of the results of these poor health conditions is that blacks over seventy represent a "biological elite and have a longer life expectancy than whites of the same age" (Linn, Hunter, and Perry 1979, p. 279). This increased life expectancy has been referred to as the "crossover effect." Research on the causes of death among black and white elderly is beginning to provide greater understanding of this phenomenon.

Among American Indians the situation is even worse. Only 6 percent of the total American population lacks indoor plumbing in their homes, but among Indians this figure is over 25 percent. Sixteen percent of Indians live in overcrowded housing with seven or more individuals (American Indian Nurses Association 1978). The effect of these poor environmental conditions is clearly shown by some major health indices. The leading diagnosis of hospitalized elderly Indians is pneumonia, a condition authors on Indian affairs attribute to environmental factors. Diabetes is the second leading disease category among elderly Indians who are treated in hospitals. The poor state of health care for Indians is shown by the high rate of amputation for gangrene related to diabetes. Poor health and living conditions are also reflected in a life expectancy of only sixty-three years for American Indians, as compared with an average of approximately seventy years for all nonwhites and seventy-four years for whites.

Because of data problems already mentioned, it is hard to outline the health or living conditions among the varied white ethnic aged groups. The type of information available is subjective data obtained by asking ethnic aged people about their health on a scale of poor to excellent. Using this approach, Guttmann (1979) found that seven groups of elderly eastern Europeans in the Baltimore-Washington area expressed satisfaction with their income and lifestyles and regarded their health as good. As we shall see later, evaluating the meaning of such expressed satisfaction is complex. There is increasing evidence that subjective evaluation by the elderly of their health status is highly correlated with objective medical tests. At this point, based on studies of elderly ethnic whites, we can surmise that the living conditions and health status of such people are better than those of their nonwhite counterparts. Continued research that provides us with solid data on these and other important indices of living conditions will enable us to validate or refute this premise.

History, Culture, and the Ethnic Aged

If the data on socioeconomic and demographic characteristics of many groups of ethnic aged people appear weak, the problems are even more severe in the area of sociocultural and psychological characteristics. The current research on these characteristics is beginning to provide us with data on attitudes and behaviors of elderly members of various ethnic groups.

Understanding attitudes and behaviors requires placing them in a framework that includes both the individual's personal history and the history of the ethnic group. The demands of migrant labor on Mexican-Americans could not fail to shape their behavior and attitudes toward growing older. Japanese who lived through the internment camps of World War II had experiences that altered traditional familial patterns. Jews who survived the holocaust were forced to reassess many of their traditional values and attitudes toward other ethnic groups. There can thus be little argument with Moore's (1971) contention that we must carefully examine history when focusing on ethnic older people.

The middle-aged Japanese-American who was interned in camps in California after 1941 was not a child whose attitudes were in the process of formation. Instead, he or she was an adult with years of experience of having lived within a strong Asian culture with well-defined norms and values. Camp living required alterations in some traditional behaviors. The actual events of the wartime period were perceived and interpreted by camp residents in terms of Japanese culture.

Life experiences are screened through the norms, beliefs, and values of a culture. For example, traditional Italian culture supposedly stresses a fatalistic stance emphasizing that many events are outside the control of the individual. Thus, Italians adhering to this stance should explain events in their life differently from Jews, who emphasize mastery by the individual over the environment. Similarly, using a model originally proposed by anthropologist Florence Kluckhohn, Tomasi (1971) has charted the differences in value orientations of Italian-Americans and Anglo-Americans (Figure 1).

Theories on Aging and Ethnic Aged Individuals

The next step in developing an understanding of ethnicity and aging requires us to relate approaches such as Tomasi's to cur-

Table 2

Contrasting Value Orientations of Italian-Americans and Anglo-Americans

Subculture	Man-Nature	Time	Activity	Relational
Italian-American	Subjugation to nature	Present	Being	Collateral
Anglo-American	Mastery over nature	Future	Doing	Individualistic

Source: Reprinted by permission from Lydio Tomasi, *The Italian-American Family* (New York: Center for Migration Studies, 1972), p. 20.

rent theoretical approaches in gerontology. Unfortunately, these approaches remain inadequate because of a variety of deficiencies.

The double-jeopardy model already cited is not a theoretical explanation per se but a description of existing conditions. Double or multiple jeopardy among ethnic aged people may result from society's demands that older individuals be removed from positions of authority so that younger individuals are able to succeed them. The demands for intergenerational transfers of power and authority may coincide with an existing subordinate status of ethnic groups such as blacks or native Americans. As subordinate members of the society, these ethnic-group members may be forced to undertake important but distasteful tasks over which they exert little or no control.

We can view this subordination in terms of either functionalist or conflict theories. Both of these theoretical approaches emphasize the mechanisms that hold society together. In functionalist terms, an unintegrated social system cannot survive. Integration motivates individuals to carry out roles needed to maintain the system. Integration also helps the social system avoid the development of cultural patterns that are too demanding for the individual or that create conflict and deviance. The basic mechanism for achieving an integrated social system is institutionalization of a system of roles. As a society develops, roles that have already emerged become institutionalized into the cultural system. The schools and parental teaching socialize children to the roles that are acceptable within the culture.

The roles that functionalists view as integrative for older individuals are those that involve their withdrawal from positions of power and authority. As stated, this withdrawal of the older person allows younger individuals with more recent training or more physical dexterity to occupy important positions.

Coming into a society with well-defined roles, ethnic groups may become integrated at the society's lowest possible level because of their lack of skills. The work they perform at this level—for example as migrant workers or domestics—may still be functional for the total society. But elderly people within these ethnic groups may find old age the hardest time of their lives, since their working years do not allow them to build up the resources they will need to face their withdrawal from the work role.

Conflict theorists also focus on integration, but see ethnic stratification as a result of the ability of some ethnic groups to mobilize power in order to attain high status and develop social boundaries between themselves and other, subordinate ethnic groups. The general relegation of older ethnic people to subordinate positions indicates the inability of these people to consolidate their position in American society and stave off the discrimination and prejudice of dominant groups.

Structural functionalism and conflict theory are widely used in social science, but have only recently been brought into theoretical analyses in social gerontology. In the 1960s gerontology was dominated by a reductionistic model that predicted that older persons would show signs of increased interest in their internal psychological states and lessened interest in the world around them. In structural-functional terms this turning inward would reflect what American society has long viewed as the optimal state for the elderly, who should "act their age" and withdraw from an active involvement in work or community affairs. It would also allow important social roles to be enacted and enable older people to get as much life satisfaction as possible in roles they have been socialized to believe are inherent in old age. As Dowd (1980) has argued, it is not difficult for the society to relegate old persons to a subordinate position, because they lack important resources to exchange in order to remain valued members of the culture. Mandatory retirement laws which were in place until 1978 helped to ensure that aged people were placed in a position of reduced power and authority in American society.

The adoption of a "disengagement" approach by social scientists in the 1960s was not explicitly based on America's negative valuation of older adults. Instead, it was supposedly based on the belief that a turning inward was vital in order to establish a psychological equilibrium on the part of individuals faced with old age and death. Disengagement was presented as an essential element of the aging process, which resulted in people whose elderly lives were spent engaging in the three R's—reading, rocking, and resting (University of Maryland 1975–76). As Hochschild (1975) observed in her critical analysis of the disengagement approach, the manner in which disengagement was presented made it almost impossible to refute. Individuals who did not disengage but rather maintained an

active interest in worldly matters were branded as "failed disen-
gagers" rather than as successful engagers.

An opposing approach, which stresses activity rather than
disengagement as characteristic of "successful" aging, has also proven
to have problems in both validity and testability. During the 1970s
gerontologists shifted toward a view that aging is part of the devel-
opmental process. From this perspective, the continuity of behavior
and attitudes on the part of elderly people would be the most
important aspect of their lives. The importance of continuity or
discontinuity is being tested in current gerontological research.
However, if continuity theory is becoming a dominant psychological
approach, stratificational approaches have become increasingly important for sociological analyses in gerontology.

The Subculture of the Aged

In the 1960s a major issue for discussion was Arnold
Rose's contention that the use of age as a prominent basis for
stratification in American society would gradually produce a subculture of the aging. Rose's belief that such a subculture was a distinct
possibility for the future rests on a number of premises. Most important to Rose's argument was the belief that the proportion of aged
people within the American population would continue to increase.
Not only would the number of elderly continue to climb, but most of
these older individuals would be retired, since mandatory retirement
appeared to be increasing. These retired individuals would be living
independently rather than intergenerational families. The fourth and
fifth supports for Rose's analyses were health factors: Advances in
medicine would enable many older individuals to reach sixty-five
with good physical health, but Rose concluded that these same individuals would also be likely to have serious chronic illnesses that
would require extensive medical treatment and increase the older
person's dependency on others for assistance. Faced with all of these
problems, Rose noted, many elderly people had internalized the idea
that the older person is of less value than the younger one; but he
also noted a "growing minority of older persons exhibiting a desire to
associate with fellow agers, especially in formal associations, and to
exclude younger adults from these associations" (1962, p. 125).

The Lack of Subcultural Development

Almost two decades after this article was published, it is
difficult to view Rose's forecast of a developing subculture of aging

adults as correct. Even Rose appeared to have reservations about his approach:

> In one sense, we hypothesize, older people may be more involved in a general culture than are middle-aged persons; this is in that older people lose some of the other subcultural variations—based on class, region, sex, and possibly even ethnic identification—characteristic of the middle-aged population. . . . They are somewhat more likely to unite on the basis of age than on the basis of these other divisions, relatively speaking, and thus the aging subculture is a more general one than are the subcultures found among the rest of the adult society. On the other hand, for some of the elderly, perhaps for those who had been socially mobile, there may be regression to earlier ethnic and class characteristics. (1962, p. 24)

The reasons a solidified group consciousness has not developed among the elderly may in part be attributed to a number of positive changes in American society. Elderly people have increased in numbers, but the numbers of older adults who have chronic illnesses and are totally dependent on someone else for assistance have not increased drastically. While the numbers of retired elderly people have increased, there has also been a major effort to change mandatory retirement laws, including the passage of the Age Discrimination Act in 1978. Retirement does not necessarily produce the "aging group consciousness" that Rose predicted. A recent study of retirement communities (Longino, McClelland, and Peterson 1980) found that residents preferred to associate with others their own age, but showed no political activism based on age.

Ironically the strongest argument against Rose's prediction can be obtained by standing it on its head. The marked increase in the population of the elderly has also been accompanied by a drop in the birthrate. This has produced a rise in the median age of the American population. With this rise has come a growing interest in the problems of the elderly. Larger numbers of professionals and paraprofessionals are finding themselves working in service organizations dedicated to the aging or in organizations such as hospitals that have a growing clientele of aged people. The "youth culture" and the devaluation of age may thus be giving way to an appreciation of the older person. As the number of older people increases and members of organizations and communities age, the older population is viewed less as a special group than as merely an intrinsic part of the American social structure. Important distinctions are thus beginning to be made between sixty-year-old persons and eighty-year-old persons. Health status has become an increasingly utilized variable for discriminating among older adults and assessing their needs.

Identity of the Older Individual

What will characterize the older individual is not necessarily the "regression" to earlier ethnic and class factors that Rose saw as a possibility, but the maintenance of those characteristics that were always important to him or her. On one level, the individual may be aware of his or her ethnic background and consciously decide to identify with it. At a second level, growing up in a particular ethnic culture may result in the individual's internalization of attitudes and values of that culture irrespective of his or her identification with these roots, and maintainence of these values into old age.

Individuals who do not identify with the ethnic culture may also not belong to any ethnic organization. They may live in a heterogeneous neighborhood and have friends from many ethnic groups. This style of life could effectively insulate a person from association with ethnic peers. The difficult question for researchers is the extent to which the life-style also means that the individual is not maintaining an ethnic identity through a variety of behaviors. Greeley has summarized the importance of this point in discussing his beliefs about the future of ethnicity:

> I am convinced that certain ethnic traits can be passed on through the early childhood socialization process whereby a child learns role expectations in relation to parents, siblings, cousins, aunts and uncles, close friends. Indeed, . . . I think this may be the most important aspect of ethnic heritage, and it is not less important because it can occur without conscious concern for such transmission on the part of parents or children. (1972, p. 8)

In Chapter 4 we will return to the issue of the transmission of ethnic values in an effort to assess the continuing importance of ethnicity for present and future cohorts of older persons.

Social-Psychological Changes and the Ethnic Aged

Since disengagement has failed to provide a global explanation of the aging process, researchers have also tended to dismiss the possibility that older persons may have lessened interest in the world around them. Cohler and Lieberman (1979) have tried to move into the often murky area of personality theory in order to test out the importance of "interiority" (a preoccupation with inner life) for aged Irish, Italian, and Polish people. Among their most important findings are the following.

1. Among Italian and Polish men, the interest in achievement decreases with age. This finding is consonant with the emphasis on "interiority" so often presumed to be a characteristic of growing older. Surprisingly, however, the authors found that concern with achievement increases with age among Irish men.

2. In contrast to the findings among the men, the orientation of women toward achievement increased with age. This result does not coincide at all with the supposedly strong homogeneity of aged people on personality changes.

3. Term of residence in the United States does not prove to be consistent in its effects among these ethnic groups. First-generation Italian men indicated a higher belief in an external locus of control than first-generation Irish or Polish men. Generation thus is not the key variable in explaining the beliefs of these three groups of ethnic aged people.

The researchers' explanation for these results encompasses both history and sociology. Interestingly, it is not only the history of Italians, Irish, and Poles in the United States, but also their history in Italy, Ireland, and Poland that is important.

In Italy, families rented land rather than owning separate parcels. Thus, nothing could be passed on from generation to generation. This lack of individual ownership encouraged the entire family to emigrate to the United States. While Polish peasants did own their land, their decision to emigrate to another country was also often a large family decision made with the advice of the parish church. But in Ireland, farmland was traditionally inherited by one child, not necessarily the oldest. Alternatively, the father divided the land up into small holdings for each of the children. Because the decision to move on the part of the Irish was a matter of individual initiative, the Irish who came to the United States were more likely to be concerned with the characteristics of "independence, achievement, and active mastery" (Cohler and Lieberman, p. 239) than Poles or Italians were.

The history of each of these groups' lives in their native country is thus intrinsic to the formation of what we often call the "ethnic personality." Of course, we would expect that the immigrants who made the decision to leave the familiar environment of their homeland and move to a foreign country were the most self-reliant segment of the population. Explaining the emigration of many groups solely in terms of the misery they suffered in their homeland may be an overstatement of the importance of living conditions and an underestimation of the importance of the individual personality. As Greeley has asserted about the Irish immigrants: "The Irish who migrated to the United States yielded nothing to anybody—save perhaps the Jews—in their orientation towards achievement" (1972,

p. 21). We could expect these types of assertive individuals to remain engaged with the society.

While there may have been a "legacy of serfdom" (Schooler 1972) among many immigrants to the United States, all of the ethnic whites who arrived were able to acculturate enough to attain at least the minimal mastery over the environment required for survival. Jews have been the most successful of all immigrant groups in obtaining economic stability, followed by immigrants from northern Europe and southern and eastern Europe. The Irish, who entered the growing public bureaucracies, were economically more successful than the Italians, who joined construction crews, or the Poles, who became the mainstay of heavy industries such as steel and automobile production. Not surprisingly, the mean income of the Irish respondents in the Cohler and Lieberman investigation was significantly higher than that of the other two groups. Economic success and a continued concern for achievement may be related in circular fashion. Economic success can fuel an interest in achievement, which in turn generates further economic success.

While the Cohler and Lieberman work is provocative, it stands as a unique piece of research which needs to be replicated among a variety of ethnic aged groups. Existing investigations provide us with some opportunities to discern whether the personality and behavior of many groups reflect age, ethnicity, or a combination of these two variables. Other commentators (Yancey, Ericksen, and Juliani 1976) have cautioned against viewing ethnic patterns in the United States as merely a transplantation of a life-style developed in the Old Country or, for blacks, in the rural South. Instead, they argue, ethnic cultures in the United States can be the result of an "interaction between the nature of the local community, the available economic opportunities, and the national or religious heritage of a particular group" (1976, p. 397).

Disengagement Among Japanese-Americans

Examining first-generation Japanese-Americans, Montero (1979) finds a decline in organizational memberships with increasing age. This disengagement from organizational activity may be due to physical problems related to chronic illnesses rather than to psychological changes. A real disengagement process, as stressed by Cumming and Henry (1961), should include a decline in the elderly person's interest in political and organizational affairs. Older Issei were less interested in both international politics and American politics than their younger counterparts, but a majority of the men still expressed an interest in American political affairs. What is most surprising, however, is that "regardless of age or sex, almost nine in ten of the Issei reported that they voted in one or both of the national elections" (Montero 1979, p. 201). Thus, to an important degree the Issei have altered traditional patterns and maintained sufficient feelings of responsibility towards American society to persist in voting. Disengagement must therefore be seen in culturally related terms, since what constitutes an "engaged" individual may vary among ethnic groups.

Many ethnic groups may see engagement in American society as requiring an abandonment of traditional culture. Discussing the aspirations of Chinese parents for their children, Fong notes that "Chinese parents want their children to conform to the traditional way of gentleness, manners, and willingness to acquiesce; they do not want them to follow in the foreign way of aggressiveness and competitive behavior" (1973, p. 117). If we want to evaluate the engagement of the ethnic aged we must examine their engagement in traditional ethnic culture as well as in mainstream American society. We can see some of the emphasis placed by older ethnic people on various types of involvement if we turn to an examination of their interaction patterns. This includes their interaction with communal organizations, family, and friends.

Interaction Patterns of Ethnic Aged

Aging has always been viewed as a period of loss for the individual. While this negative approach has been overstated, there is no denying that aging individuals face loss of a spouse and a shrinking circle of friends and kin. Senior citizens can create new friendships, but the deaths of individuals who have been intimates for long periods of time are not easily forgotten. Interactional choices may thus narrow as elderly people grow older, and these choices may be further constricted if such persons do not engage in activities that bring them into contact with a new group of potential friends. Even if an elderly individual does maintain extensive contact with a variety of individuals, interactions with children and relatives may become more important to him or her.

Family Proximity and the Ethnic Aged

The family is very important among ethnic older persons. Among aged blacks interviewed in the San Diego area, 19 percent had brothers or sisters in San Diego county and 6 percent had brothers or sisters in the immediate neighborhood (Sanford 1978).

Twelve percent of these elderly people had children in the county and immediate neighborhood. Elderly Japanese had roughly the same proportion of relatives in the area, but over 20 percent had children living in the same residence (Ishizuka 1978). Among elderly Latinos an even higher percentage (32 percent) had children living in the same house, and over a third had either children or grandchildren living in the immediate vicinity. Almost 90 percent of the older Mexican-Americans had some relative living in the immediate neighborhood, and over half had a relative living in the same household (Valle and Mendoza 1978).

Data are less available on the proximity of white members of ethnic groups to their relatives. In Baltimore, a sample of Polish and Italian middle-aged individuals indicated that having family members live nearby is also common among these groups: 70 percent had parents living in the same community, 48 percent had siblings in the same community, and an additional 28 percent had siblings in other parts of Baltimore (Fandetti 1974). Overall, nearly three-quarters of all older persons have a child living within a half-hour's travel time (Federal Council on the Aging 1981).

The effects of family proximity can be numerous. At a minimum, having family nearby should facilitate a high rate of interaction between the ethnic aged and other family members. To have someone to talk to on a frequent basis is a strong desire on the part of all ethnic aged people. Chinese elders in San Diego were clearly interested in increased contact with relatives (Cheng 1978). What these elderly people mean by "contact" can take many forms. It can range from phone calls and inquiries about one's health to assistance and the sharing of important emotional expressions. In recent years, gerontologists have begun to emphasize that the quantity of contacts is less important than their intensity and meaning to the individual.

Confidants and the Ethnic Aged

Lowenthal's (1968) work in San Francisco has thus had a major impact in defining the need of elderly individuals not only for extensive contacts but for a "confidant" relationship. A confidant is an individual with whom the person can share intimate thoughts, and the presence or absence of a confidant can affect an individual's well-being. The lack of a confidant may hamper the ability of the elderly to cope with personal losses.

While data on the type of individuals who perform confidant roles in ethnic cultures are lacking, the relationships among generations in various ethnic cultures indicate the types of interactions we would expect to find. Italian families, for example, stress the authority and not the warmth of the parent. Given this emphasis, it may be difficult for the elderly parent to discuss problems with even adult children. The elderly parent may feel that such openness may be seen as a sign of weakness. In cultures that stress *machismo,* the sharing of feelings and personal problems may be very difficult for men. Support and assistance, but not sharing, may thus be the characteristic interactional pattern among generations in many ethnic cultures.

Krause's (1978) investigation of three generations of women in Italian, Jewish, and Slavic families showed what she termed an "impressionistic" attitude of closeness among these generations. Over 70 percent of the elderly people in her study confided in their children. The type and degree of confiding were not determined in Krause's study, however, and need to be detailed before we can reach an assessment of the relationships characteristic of white ethnic aged women and their children.

As Montero (1979) found among elderly Japanese-Americans, visiting with friends declines with age partly because of problems with physical mobility and also because of increased mortality. If family members live reasonably near, they often become the major source of social relationships for ethnic aged people. Visiting with children by Issei in Los Angeles did not show any decline with age. The interactions with family members of elderly Mexican-Americans in Los Angeles was higher than those found among elderly whites or blacks in the same city. In contrast, these same Mexican-Americans had the least amount of interaction with non-family members, indicating a growing reliance on the family for the satisfaction of their emotional needs (Bengtson 1979). Whether the family is able to provide the intimate and confidant needs of ethnic aged people will thus vary by cultural orientation and the resources and demands placed on all of the generations in the ethnic family.

Life Satisfaction of Ethnic Aged People

Satisfaction and Family

Assessing life satisfaction is not simply a matter of tallying the interaction rates of ethnic aged individuals with a variety of kin and friends. We need to examine a number of other important topics, including feelings about their immediate neighborhood and culturally related expectations about aging.

Asking three generations of women from Italian, Jewish, and Slavic backgrounds what "makes them feel good," Krause (1978) found that almost half of the grandmothers answered "love and attention" as opposed to only 36 to 37 percent of the two younger generations. Broken down by ethnicity, the data revealed a major difference between the Jewish women and the respondents from Slavic and Italian backgrounds. Jewish women had a stronger attachment to their child's accomplishment as something that would make them feel good than women from the two other ethnic groups.

The finding that 68 percent of the oldest generation in all three groups felt that caring for their family made them feel useful is consistent with other findings. Because of the strong interest in the family among ethnic aged whites, we would expect the interest in caring for their families shown by Krause's grandmothers to be a common refrain among many white ethnic groups. The position of the elder in the family system has certainly also been stressed in Oriental culture. In black and Latino cultures, as already mentioned, grandparents are actively involved in child rearing. Indeed, as a group with limited resources, the present generation of ethnic aged people can be expected to rely extensively on interaction with their families to provide them with a sense of satisfaction with their lives.

General Satisfaction

At present, the satisfaction of most ethnic aged people would appear to be high. Despite the positive responses, probing into an area as complex as life satisfaction may produce simplistic answers. Queried about their life satisfaction, ethnic aged individuals may answer in terms of their expectations about growing older or on a basis of "given how bad things could be, life is not so bad." The latter perspective seemed to be true of all of the groups studied in the San Diego project. Only Mexican-Americans expressed enough reservations about their present living patterns to alert the interviewers to the need for further questioning. The basis for dissatisfaction among the elderly Mexican-Americans was the loss of family ties, since they viewed the "social conditions" of their lives as positive. In other words, the weakening of familial traditions decreased their satisfaction with their lives despite improvements in income benefits and services.

In New Jersey, 143 elderly black men and women who stressed a fear of going outside described "being alive" as the aspect of life they "liked best" (Faulkner, Heisel, and Simms 1975). Over one-half of these respondents described themselves as happy. Health, independence, and the well-being of their children's families were the most important components of their happiness.

A Detroit study by Jackson, Bacon, and Peterson (1977–78) interviewed aged blacks who were active in senior centers. These elderly people also stressed the importance of health to their life satisfaction. In contrast, however, a recent study of public housing residents in Cleveland (Deimling, Noelker, and Beckman 1979) noted that older black residents viewed the maintenance of social relationships rather than health as the major factor in their life satisfaction. The difference between these two studies may be an artifact of the sample populations involved. Since the older black men and women interviewed in Detroit were attempting to maintain an active involvement in senior centers, good health was vital to their daily activities. The Cleveland group may have contained individuals with more varied health statuses, including those whose illnesses made it difficult for them to attend programs such as those available at senior centers. For these older persons, the most important aspect of life may be a continued high level of interaction with friends or relatives.

In Los Angeles, researchers probed the issue of life satisfaction among Mexican-Americans, blacks, and whites by asking each group what they liked about "being the age you are." Bengtson (1979) has branded the primary responses as almost stereotypic: Elderly blacks expressed delight at being alive, Mexican-Americans at not having to work so hard, and whites at a new freedom to travel. Importantly, almost a third of both black and Mexican elderly men stressed not having to work so hard. This common feeling among two groups of minority aged people reflects differences between their economic status and the economic status of aged whites. For lower-income blacks and whites, removal from an abhorred occupation may be more important than for whites who can afford to see aging as a time to engage in activities that were previously limited because of tight work schedules.

Neighborhood Satisfaction

There can be little question that for most older individuals, the immediate environment will be more important than it was during a previous period of active daily work. Many older people give up their driver's licenses because of increasing vision problems. Lacking the ability to drive, they must then be dependent on the inadequate mass transportation system of most cities, if they live in an urban area. With the onset of chronic illness, even making use of available mass transit may become difficult. The older individual thus often lacks the physical mobility of younger adults and becomes more dependent on the immediate environment to satisfy a variety of needs.

An attachment to local communities has, however, always

been seen as a characteristic of the ethnic working class. In the 1940s Firey (1945) published an important paper stressing the symbolic meaning of geographic areas to residents. In 1963 Fried noted the grief among many Italian families who were being forced to relocate from Boston's West End because of an impending urban renewal project.

For ethnic older persons the neighborhood represents the site where much of their social interaction takes place and where the homes of a large proportion of their children, relatives, and friends are. Dense ethnic communities provide elderly individuals with compatriots who share values, norms, and a common language. Montero (1979) notes the high percentage of Issei who belong to communal organizations. In Milwaukee, Biegel and Sherman (1979) found a high degree of organizational affiliation among white ethnic aged people. Extensive involvement in community organizations does not mean that aged members of ethnic groups are more interested in community issues than members of other groups are. Instead, as Fandetti observes, "Members of the ethnic neighborhood participate in community associations, mainly because they serve the purpose of providing additional opportunities for informal social activities, rather than cooperative work aimed at the accomplishment of abstract goals" (1978, p. 51).

Criminal activities that force the elderly person to stay barricaded inside the home are very serious for ethnic older persons. McAdoo's (1979) study of elderly blacks living in public and private housing in Washington, D.C., showed that a fear of crime had forced many of these elderly to be "cautious" about activities and to cut down on visiting with friends or relatives and on attendance at church or other social activities. In short, a fear of crime was producing a pattern of isolation.

Moving to a new community would be financially and physically difficult for many of these black elderly people. Moving would also cut them off from the contacts that are so important in the ethnic community. In many neighborhoods, ethnic aged worked for years at low-paying jobs to be able to purchase their homes. The equity they now have in these residences would not allow them to purchase an equivalent home in the inflated housing markets of the 1980s.

Attachment to a home and the presence of children, relatives, and long-time friends are major reasons for remaining in a community. These feelings are reflected in Milwaukee, where the majority of ethnic aged whites viewed their neighborhood as satisfactory. As Biegel and Sherman note, "Over half of the interviewees (58.1 percent) stated that they saw their neighborhood as a place where they really belonged" (1979, p. 327).

Expectations about Aging

Despite the stated satisfaction of the ethnic aged with their lives, there are differences in the level of satisfaction among the ethnic groups. One explanation for these differences may be the varied expectations about aging among the ethnic elderly. Financial security, optimal living conditions, and good health are certainly important elements in enabling anyone to lead a satisfying life. The way in which these different pieces fit together in a total "life satisfaction score" may be strongly related to the expectations of diverse ethnic groups.

Jews, for example, have been among the most economically successful groups in the United States. We would surmise that life satisfaction for many middle-class Jews would be related to their ability to maintain in old age the status they attained and the style of life they pursued while working. Given Krause's (1978) findings of an emphasis on the children's success, we can also expect middle-class aged Jews to be satisfied if their children are successful. An aspect of this orientation is that Jewish aged people demand less often that their children maintain the high frequency of contact that some other ethnic aged groups expect.

The family also remains the cornerstone of existence for Mormons. As Gelfand and Olsen (1979) explain, "The Mormon belief is that postmortal existence is based on an extended family kinship network. If one does not have an affiliation on this earth with such a system, progress after death cannot occur. The family is the basic social organization in the eternal Kingdom of God" (1979, p. 214). We would thus expect the coherence of the family to be crucial to the elderly Mormons' assessment of their present status.

Among elderly Asians, life satisfaction may revolve around the degree to which they are able to move into the role of the "honorable elder," a role in which they are awarded respect and authority from younger family members. Ragan and Bengtson (1979) found lower levels of life satisfaction among aged Mexican-Americans than among blacks and whites in Los Angeles. The elderly Mexican-Americans were also the most vociferous in their complaints about the decline in family life. As the researchers concluded, "While at an objective level the older Mexican-American may be no more socially isolated than the white older person, he may well be isolated at a subjective level as evidenced by his significantly lower morale in a situation of unmet expectations" (1977, p. 99).

Unfulfilled expectations may lower the satisfaction of ethnic aged people whatever their objective living situation may be. It is also possible, however, that such people have limited expectations about their later life. Jackson (1970) and Ward (1979) have noted that elderly blacks have lower life expectancies, perceive of themselves as being "old" at an earlier age than whites, and are in worse physiological condition than whites. Concurrent with the perception of being older, however, may be a more positive attitude toward later life and an unaggressive and undemanding attitude toward this stage of the life cycle (Ward 1979). As Dancy (1977) argues, the importance of religion in the lives of blacks also deserves continuing attention as a component in life satisfaction. Older blacks attend church more frequently than older whites (Ward 1979), but little evidence exists to support the stereotype that black aged people immerse themselves in fundamentalist religious groups.

We must also not forget that blacks now in their seventies and eighties experienced discrimination which restricted their opportunity to enter old age with any income security or a health status comparable to that of their white age peers. As Jackson, Bacon, and Peterson have noted, the limitations placed on blacks by racism may be a vital factor in lowering their expectations of life in general and of old age in particular:

> It is conceivable that the effects of age discrimination, loss of esteem structures (work, income, status, social contacts) and other attendant consequences of aging in this society might have different or more negative contrast effects upon such social psychological constructs as life satisfaction for whites than blacks. The relative influence of such negative occurrences on the life satisfaction of blacks might be incrementally less or have different antecedents or correlates due to the omnipresence of discrimination and social inequality in the environment prior to and during the aging period. (1977–78, p. 177)

Given the negative attitudes toward aging that exist in American society, it would be unreasonable to expect any ethnic group to have a totally positive attitude toward growing old. While the elderly in many ethnic groups may have occupied positions of power in their countries of origin, there are few indications that these ethnic groups are prepared to accord them such positions of authority in the United States.

For example, the reports of Montero (1979) and Kiefer (1974) indicate that the role of the elderly family member among Japanese families may be changing as Nisei (second-generation Americans) and Sansei (third-generation Americans) move closer to "American" values. Wu (1975), examining Chinese-Americans in Los Angeles, noted a reduction in the social status of elderly people, as children became more important than parents in the extended family. Ethnic aged people may be able to anticipate respect from their adult children and their grandchildren, but they cannot necessarily expect any authority comparable to what they might have obtained in the Old Country.

Ethnicity and Longevity

As we have seen, attitudes toward death are related to what ethnic groups view as the natural course of their life span. The evidence, however, remains inconclusive on factors that determine longevity. There are constant reports of individuals in remote areas of Europe and Asia with incredibly long life spans and high activity levels until their death. In some cases their longevity has been attributed to climate, diet, or genetic superiority. Work habits and freedom from the stresses of modern living or the communicable diseases of modern urbanized culture have also been thrown into the hopper as explanations.

Eliminating any of these explanations is not yet possible. Indications are also increasing that research about some of these long-lived people is based on questionable evidence about the actual age of the older adults within these groups. The anthropologist who is told that a particular individual is 113 may actually be encountering an eighty-year-old man or woman.

In the United States differences exist in the availability of quality health care and in health-care practices that are related to longevity. Jews have higher rates of heart problems than other ethnic groups, which could be attributed to the high socioeconomic status of Jews and the stressful white-collar positions they occupy, or to the high-cholesterol diets they tend to enjoy. Blacks over the age of seventy-five appear to be in better physical condition and to live longer than whites of a comparable age. This positive finding about elderly blacks may in part be attributed to the different genetic endowments of whites and blacks. Unfortunately, fewer blacks than whites survive to seventy-five because of major socioeconomic problems and the poorer health care this minority group generally receives. Blacks who reach seventy-five are, by a process of elimination, the most physically and perhaps the most psychologically fit of the elderly blacks.

Pulling together these varied explanations is a task for biological and social research over the next few decades. Even if biological and genetic endowments are found to account for two-thirds of an individual's expected longevity, it remains for us to explain the remaining percentages. It is possible that certain types of individuals with specific personality makeups are better able to cope with the demands of growing older and therefore survive for a longer period of time. Studies of the adjustment of individuals to relocation in nursing homes, for instance, indicates that individuals who are aggressive and seek to explore their environment and utilize the home to its fullest measure adjust more quickly and survive the longest (Tobin and Lieberman 1976). In Chicago, Lieberman (1974) found that older Italians who evidenced positive well-being were more aggressive individuals. Different rates of longevity among ethnic groups may be based in part on the types of behavior reinforced by the ethnic culture and the extent to which this reinforcement aids or hinders older people in adjusting to the demands of the society in which they are living.

This presentation must remain incomplete until more data are available, but the existence of differences among ethnic aged people on a variety of dimensions, including longevity, should be clear. With these differences in mind, we can turn to an examination of how ethnic older persons fit into the existing service delivery system and the special concerns and needs that these clients pose for providers.

References

American Indian Nurses Association. 1978. *The environment of elderly native Americans.* Rockville, Md.: Indian Health Service.

Bengtson, V. 1979. Ethnicity and aging: Problems and issues in current social science inquiry. In D. Gelfand and A. Kutzik (eds.), *Ethnicity and aging.* New York: Springer.

Biegel, D., and Sherman, W. 1979. Neighborhood capacity building and the ethnic aged. In D. Gelfand and A. Kutzik (eds.), *Ethnicity and aging.* New York: Springer.

Cheng, E. 1978. *The elder Chinese.* San Diego: Center on Aging, San Diego State University.

Cohler, B., and Lieberman, M. 1979. Personality change across the second half of life: Findings from a study of Irish, Italian, and Polish-American men and women. In D. Gelfand and A. Kutzik (eds.), *Ethnicity and aging.* New York: Springer.

Cummings, E., and Henry, W. 1961. *Growing old.* New York: Basic Books.

Dancy, J. 1977. *The Black elderly.* Ann Arbor, Mich.: Institute of Gerontology.

Deimling, G., Noelker, L., and Beckman, A. 1979. The impact of race on the resources and well-being of aged public housing residents. Paper presented at meeting of the Gerontological Society, Washington, D.C., November 1979.

Dowd, J. 1980. Exchange rates and old people. *Journal of Gerontology* 35: 596–603.

Fandetti, D. 1974. Sources of assistance in a white working-class ethnic neighborhood. Unpublished Ph.D. dissertation, Columbia University, New York.

———. 1978. Ethnicity and neighborhood services. In D. Thursz and J. Vigilante (eds.), *Reaching people: The structure of neighborhood services.* Beverly Hills, Calif.: Sage.

Faulkner, A., Heisel, M., and Simms, P. 1975. Life strengths and life stresses: Explorations in the measurement of the mental health of the black aged. *American Journal of Orthopsychiatry* 45: 102–110.

Federal Council on the Aging. 1981. *The need for long term care.* Washington, D.C.: U.S. Department of Health and Human Services.

Fong, S. 1973. Assimilation and changing social roles of Chinese-Americans. *Journal of Social Issues* 29: 115–27.

Fowles, D. 1978. *Statistical reports on older Americans: Some prospects for the future elderly population.* Washington, D.C.: Administration on Aging, National Clearinghouse on Aging.

Gelfand, D., and Olsen, J. 1979. Aging in the Jewish and Mormon family. In D. Gelfand and A. Kutzik (eds.), *Ethnicity and aging.* New York: Springer.

Guttmann, D. 1979. Use of informal and formal supports by the ethnic aged. In D. Gelfand and A. Kutzik (Eds.), *Ethnicity and aging.* New York: Springer.

Hill, R. 1978. A demographic profile of the black aged. *Aging,* Nos. 287–288: 2–9.

Hochschild, A. 1975. Disengagement theory: A critique and proposal. *American Sociological Review* 40: 553–69.

Ishizuka, K. 1978. *The elder Japanese.* San Diego: Center on Aging, San Diego State University.

Jackson, J. J. 1970. Aged Negroes and their cultural departures from statistical stereotypes and rural-urban differences. *Gerontologist* 10: 140–45.

———. 1978. Special health problems of aged blacks. *Aging* 287–288: 15–20.

Jackson, J., Bacon, J., and Peterson, J. 1977–78. Life satisfaction among black urban elderly. *International Journal of Aging and Human Development* 8: 169–80.

Kiefer, C. 1974. *Changing cultures, changing lives.* San Francisco: Jossey-Bass.

Krause, C. 1978. *Grandmothers, mothers and daughters.* New York: Institute on Pluralism and Group Identity.

Lieberman, M. 1974. Adaptational patterns in middle-aged and elderly: The role of ethnicity. Paper presented at meeting of the Gerontological Society, Portland, Ore., November 1974.

Linn, M., Hunter, K., and Perry, P. 1979. Differences by sex and ethnicity in the psychosocial adjustment of the elderly. *Journal of Health and Social Behavior,* 20: 278–281.

Longino, C., McClelland, K., and Peterson, W. 1980. The aged subculture hypothesis: Social integration, gerontophilia and self-conception. *Journal of Gerontology,* 35: 758–767.

Lowenthal, M. 1968. Social isolation and mental illness in old age. In B. Neugarten (ed.), *Middle-age and aging.* Chicago: University of Chicago Press.

McAdoo, J. 1979. Fear of crime and well-being of black elderly. In D. Gelfand and A. Kutzik (eds.), *Ethnicity and aging.* New York: Springer.

Montero, D. 1979. Disengagement and aging among the Issei. In D. Gelfand and A. Kutzik (eds.), *Ethnicity and aging.* New York: Springer.

Moore, J. 1971. Mexican-Americans. *Gerontologist* 11, pt. II: 30–35.

Peterson, R. 1978. *The elder Filipino.* San Diego: Center on Aging, San Diego State University.

Ragan, P., and Bengtson, B. 1977. *Aging among blacks, Mexican-Americans and whites: Developments, procedures and results of the community survey.* Los Angeles: Andrus Gerontology Center, University of Southern California.

Rich, S. 1979. Hidden poor among the elderly. *Washington Post,* April 14, 1979, A-2.

Rose, A. 1962. The subculture of the aging. *Gerontologist* 2: 123–27.

Sanford, P. 1978. *The elder black.* San Diego: Center on Aging, San Diego State University.

Schooler, C. 1976. Serfdom's legacy: An ethnic continuum. *American Journal of Sociology* 81: 1265–85.

Thernstrom, S. 1973. *The other Bostonians.* Cambridge: Harvard University Press.

Tobin, S., and Lieberman, M. 1976. *Last home for the aged.* San Francisco: Jossey-Bass.

Tomasi, L. 1972. *The Italian-American family.* New York: Center for Migration Studies.

U.S. Bureau of the Census. 1978. *Social and economic characteristics of the older population, 1978.* Current Population Reports, Series P-23, no. 85, Washington, D.C.

U.S. Senate, Special Committee on Aging. 1980. *Every ninth American.* Washington, D.C.

University of Maryland. 1975–76. Mrs. Adams. Tape C-6 in *Aging: The human experience.* College Park, Md.: Center on Aging.

Urban Resources Consultants. 1978. *Issue paper on the minority aging.* Washington, D.C.

Valle, R., and Mendoza, L. 1978. *The elder Latino.* San Diego: San Diego State University.

Ward, R. 1979. Minority aging: Double jeopardy or leveling? Paper presented at the meeting of the Gerontological Society, Washington, D.C., November 1979.

Yancey, W., Ericksen, E., and Juliani, R. 1976. Emergent ethnicity: A review and reformulation. *American Sociological Review* 41: 391–402.

Chapter

3

Serving the Ethnic Aged Population

The differences among the ethnic aged groups discussed in Chapter 2 would appear to be basic in nature, but it is only recently that many service providers have shown any sensitivity to their implications for programs and services. Aged people remain an underserved population, and ethnic aged people comprise a large portion of the elderly whose needs have yet to be met by formal or informal means. The low socioeconomic status of the ethnic aged population contributes to its extensive need for services.

Despite this need, Guttmann (1979) found minimal use of services among the seven European-based groups he studied in the Baltimore-Washington area. Among his findings:

1. Jewish elderly people used more services than any other of the ethnic groups.

2. Almost 75 percent of the Hungarians did not use any of the formal services.

3. Medicaid was used by 20 percent to 25 percent of the elderly in the Greek, Jewish, Hungarian, and Polish (Washington) groups, and to a considerably less degree by the other groups.

4. Use of food stamps was minimal.

5. Little or no use was reported for meals on wheels. (1979, p. 251)

In this chapter we will examine those characteristics of ethnic aged people that affect their participation in programs and the effectiveness of providers working in programs that serve them. We will also explore the role of ethnic aged people in providing support for each other and the assistance that can be provided by family, friends, and neighbors. Before undertaking this exploration we need to review briefly current programs and services in aging in order to integrate the programmatic discussion of this chapter.

Models of Aging Programs and Services

Until the middle 1960s few specialized services for aged people besides nursing homes existed. State mental hospitals tended to serve as de facto nursing homes. Nineteen sixty-five must be regarded as a watershed year for the development of programs and services on aging. In that year, Congress passed the Older Americans Act, which authorized services to individuals over sixty-five, and enacted the long-fought-for but controversial Medicare legislation.

The Older Americans Act authorized within the Department of Health, Education, and Welfare an Administration on Aging to coordinate aging programs. Only minimal funding for programs and services was appropriated under this legislation during the 1960s. Instead, appropriations were earmarked for demonstration projects. In 1972, however, the Nutrition Services Act authorized large-scale direct-service nutrition programs for the elderly. Once this precedent for direct funding had been set, substantial amounts of funds began to flow into other service areas for older citizens. In the same year the age limitation on populations eligible for services under the Older Americans Act was dropped from sixty-five to sixty with little opposition from Congress. This change increased the number of individuals who could benefit from expanded aging programs and services.

Since 1975, when the Older Americans Act was amended for the seventh time, the increase in funding for such programs and services has been substantial. The budget for the Administration on Aging in 1965 totaled $7 million. This had grown to $550 million in 1978. Many of the programs now available are an outgrowth of the demonstration programs begun in the 1960s. Others are the result of concerns about the effectiveness of existing services.

Given the increased options in services that older people with varying needs have, we again need to shift our attention to an examination of aged members of ethnic groups. In contrast to the previous chapter, we will now focus our attention on the economic, psychological, and cultural characteristics that will affect the organizational approach and components of a program intent on obtaining extensive participation among ethnic people.

The Effects of Ethnicity on Service Usage

It is important to keep in mind that a broad discussion of this kind may gloss over the numerous variations of characteristics. In the case of the ethnic aged population, these variations may be rooted in both individual personality and the generation to which the individual belongs. First-generation immigrants to the United States may have maintained a style of life comparable to what they observed in the Old Country. With increased acculturation many people may alter their attachment to the traditional culture, and these changes may show up most strongly among the second-, third-, and fourth-generation Americans of the ethnic group. As this discussion progresses, we will pay some attention to these important generational differences.

Factors that need to be taken into account in the planning, implementation, and day-to-day operation of programs and services for the elderly include:

1. Lack of knowledge on the part of ethnic aged people about cultures other than their own;

2. Lack of knowledge among ethnic aged people of available services;

3. Lack of utilization by ethnic aged people of available services;

4. Unwillingness of ethnic aged people to travel beyond certain defined neighborhood boundaries, and unavailability of adequate transportation to services;

5. Low expectation of services;

6. Strong preferences among ethnic aged people for the maintenance of ethnic culture.

Lack of Knowledge of Other Cultures

Growing up in a neighborhood environment that has a high density of ethnic individuals may isolate the older person from young and middle-aged individuals from other ethnic groups. This is expecially true in communities that possess what Breton (1964) has termed "institutional completeness," that is, a range of institutions that are able to provide totally for the needs of the individual.

The importance of contact among ethnic and racial groups has been recurrently stressed by sociologists attempting to explain the presence or absence of harmonious intergroup relations. If positive attitudes toward other cultures exist and there is an absence of entrenched stereotypes, contact among ethnic groups can be an important step toward improving intercultural relations. This contact, however, must be on a basis of equality between the groups, rather than of one group's superiority to the other.

In dense ethnic communities, an individual's primary contact is with his or her own kind rather than with members of other ethnic groups. If residents of "Little Italy" do encounter blacks from outside the neighborhood, the encounter is not likely to be on an equal-status basis; the blacks are likely to be working as domestics. For many blacks in New York, the major encounter with Jews has been with Jewish storeowners in the black community. These Jewish merchants have often been seen as exploitative and usurious. In Washington, D.C., the major contact of residents with newly arrived Koreans is with those Koreans who have become owners of small grocery stores in poorer communities.

Formulations of attitudes about other cultures on the basis of these kinds of limited and not always positive contacts can be difficult to change. Although people can receive extensive information about ethnic groups through educational programs, this information may not jibe with personal contacts. As a result, the information is often simply ignored.

Limited interethnic contacts are characteristic of immigrants who arrived in the United States during the 1890s and early 1900s. For many of these groups, the best employment opportunities appeared to be in occupations in which their countrymen were already working. As already noted, problems with English also encouraged them to settle into ethnic neighborhoods. While Jews and Italians often found work in companies operated by fellow ethnic-group members, the employers of blacks, Chicanos, and other minorities were always white. Disagreements between employees and employers were often exacerbated by cultural and racial differences, such as different valuations of work, punctuality, or the pace at which work should be performed.

Because of higher education and better job prospects, the second- and third-generation ethnic individual has had increased opportunities to interact with other ethnic groups on an equal status. This has been especially true in the last thirty years. Whatever the monetary value of a college education, one of its most important functions has been to bring locally oriented youths out of their close-knit ethnic communities into a more diverse college atmosphere. As the "baby boom" generation ages, we can expect to find ethnic aged people with more varied interethnic experiences both in their general interactions and in their work relationships.

Lack of Knowledge of Available Services

Guttmann (1979) attributes the low service utilization rate of ethnic aged whites to their lack of knowledge of what services are available. Ignorance of services may also reflect disinterest on the part of service providers; it has been evident for some time that outreach has not been a top priority among many programs. Even if outreach is undertaken, ethnic aged people may not be interested in learning about programs which they perceive as being run by outsiders. Whether it is correct or not, this attitude may be based on the perception that outsiders do not and cannot understand the needs of particular ethnic groups.

Unwillingness to Utilize Services

Many of the present ethnic older persons as first-generation Americans, engaged in intensive struggles to survive before coming to the United States, and these struggles continued after their arrival in this country. These senior citizens are rightfully proud of their ability to conquer all hurdles with assistance only from nuclear and extended family members. They may thus view services not as helpful adjuncts to their own resources, but as tantamount to charity. Additionally, they may see a number of services as stigmatizing. This is especially true of mental health services; the elderly currently represent only 4 percent of the caseload of community mental health centers and 2 percent of the time of private psychiatrists (Berkman 1978).

In general, it appears that the present generation of elderly citizens are reluctant to use services. The General Accounting Office found in a study in Cleveland (Comptroller General of the United States 1977) that few of the elderly who were interviewed recognized their needs for such programs, despite extensive impairment of their ability to carry out important daily functions. As Guttmann (1979) notes, securing utilization of services by ethnic elderly persons requires more than simply informing them about what is available. Education about the services and a major effort to dispel beliefs about them as charity are also necessary.

Unwillingness to Travel to Services

To the individual entrenched in the local ethnic community, the outside world may be any location not in the immediate neighborhood. "Outside" may be threatening merely because it is unfamiliar. On the other hand, this outside world may be threatening because it contains individuals who are "different." Fear of the larger environment may be heightened among individuals whose knowledge of English is limited, who have difficulty reading signs, or whose physical strength and ambulatory ability are limited. It should therefore not be surprising that a Polish woman in her eighties expresses reservations about attending a program or going to a medical clinic in another community, especially if she has no familiarity with the subway or bus systems, or finds negotiating the high steps of a bus physically difficult.

Lack of Available Transportation

A recent conference emphasized the inability of many elderly blacks to reach medical centers (Davis et al. 1977). Inadequate medical services have always been a problem in black communities, since the predominantly white medical profession has chosen to practice in more affluent localities. The fee-for-service medical system of the United States has also discouraged the location of adequate medical services in communities where lower-income ethnic aged predominate. While the community mental health center approach has been a step in the right direction, most voluntary agencies do not provide localized services to older members of ethnic groups.

The ethnic aged individual's reliance on family members for primary assistance may be beneficial to family integration, but it may also make the older person tend to rely on family members for aid in reaching medical and social services outside of the neighborhood. Specialized transportation programs are now attempting to take the elderly to services, often giving top priority to reaching medical facilities.

Low Expectation of Services

For many ethnic older persons past experiences with services have been unsatisfactory. While the seemingly endless bureaucratic maze that often appears to be intrinsic to social services can be confusing to anyone, the forms and rules are even more confusing to an older individual with limited literacy or fluency in English. If we compound these deficits with vision or hearing problems as well as minimal access to transportation, we can understand why many ethnic aged people do not utilize services.

If they attempt to do so, they may be befuddled by problems of eligibility. Whether "means testing" is a valid concept is not important here. What is crucial is that we realize that means testing reinforces the impression of elderly people that services are charity rather than something to which they are entitled. Fortunately, programs run under the authority of the Administration on Aging have no means-testing requirements. Area Agencies on Aging, which administer many of the services, are required to give priority in funding to geographic areas that have elderly residents with the greatest economic and social needs.

The belief that the recipient of services should be "deserving and grateful" is often reinforced by providers who are insensitive to cultural differences or simply rude to older ethnic men and women. This is especially true in agencies that are overloaded with cases. Workers in these settings often find the special attention required by older adults frustrating and time-consuming. Faced with bureaucratic regulations and frustrated by the impatience or indifference of service providers, older adults may come to the conclusion that they cannot expect to obtain any quality services. Service providers who are genuinely concerned about senior citizens may find the low expectations of the ethnic aged population an obstacle to obtaining high levels of participation in their programs.

Preference to Maintain Ethnic Culture

Utilization of local service providers or natural helpers may reflect not only an attachment to the community, but a desire by older persons to carry on the traditional culture. They may view nonethnic professionals as a threat to their traditional manner of dealing with problems. This belief is not totally unfounded. Practitioners who are not from the same ethnic culture may attempt to deal with problems in ways that are inimical to that culture or that encourage the elderly individual to change long-ingrained and culturally related habits. These could include major changes in diet, residential location, or traditional relationships with other family members. It should therefore not be surprising that an elderly ethnic-group member turns to community-based helpers or his or her own family for assistance.

Keeping all of these diverse considerations in mind when working with ethnic older persons is difficult but necessary. A consistent focus on these factors will have an impact on some important decisions that service providers have to make during the planning and development stages, including the location of programs, the auspices under which they are operated, composition of the staff, staff/client ratios, and actual program components. As we consider each of these elements, we can relate the characteristics of the ethnic aged population to specific program components.

Ethnic Older Persons and Program Development

Location of Programs and Services

An organization may be able to choose among a number of available sites from which to run a new program or service. In some areas of the country, services for the aged are being offered in recycled rather than newly constructed buildings, such as schools that had been closed because of lack of enrollment, old fire stations, or even unused train stations. Organizations often base their decision to utilize a particular space on the costs of construction or renovation and on proximity of the site to mass transportation. Plans to locate a service for the ethnic aged population must consider issues that go beyond physical factors.

Location of a service outside the ethnic older person's neighborhood may be unacceptable to the elderly since it would require them to travel outside the area they regard as theirs. Even if mass transportation or a special transportation program is in operation, traveling outside the neighborhood may force the older individual to interact with members of other cultures. While many practitioners may regard this as a worthwhile experience, the older adult from a strong ethnic community may not see it in the same way.

Unfortunately, a program or service located so as to minimize the travel of its ethnic aged clients may not be cost-efficient because of the small number of senior citizens in the neighborhood. On the other hand, locating the program in an area not associated with one particular ethnic group may result in a lack of utilization by a significant number of older people.

Auspices

Location is not the only determinant of success of a program. Decisions about program auspices may also attract particular groups of aged people and deter others from attending a senior center. Programs for the ethnic aged population can be run under the auspices of voluntary organizations, local commissions on aging, county or local government, or sectarian organizations. In some communities the church may be the most acceptable provider of services for aged people, since it has been stressed as a vital link in their lives.

Although there has been criticism of sociologists' emphasis on religiosity, Dancy (1977) has recently reemphasized the importance of the church to aged blacks. Besides its religious components, the church may be highly valued and respected as an institution by older members of ethnic and minority groups. Among middle-aged Italians and Poles in Baltimore and Italians in the suburb of Columbia, Maryland, the majority preferred the Catholic church over alternative organizations as the agency to run nursing homes (Fandetti and Gelfand 1976; Gelfand and Fandetti 1980). The church was chosen by these individuals because they saw it as the provider of the highest-quality services. A substantial percentage (29 percent) of the Baltimore sample preferred nursing homes under the auspices of a local ethnic organization. In Columbia, however, respondents did not view an ethnic organization as a potential service provider, and many of the men in the study expressed a preference for nursing homes run by private, proprietary, profit-making organizations.

The proportion of individuals preferring church-sponsored services is not the same among different generations of ethnic whites. First-generation immigrant Italians and Poles in Baltimore expressed a preference for government-sponsored programs, while second- and third-generation Americans were more attuned to programs under church auspices. This surprising result has at least two possible explanations. First, the middle-aged first-generation immigrants from southern and eastern Europe come from societies where extensive government services are the norm and thus expect services provided by the federal, state, and local governments in this country to be widely available and of high quality. Second, middle-aged second- and third-generation adults may have had negative experiences with government-run services and now associate them with welfare.

It thus seems reasonable to predict that services under the auspices of church groups and private firms may achieve a higher degree of participation from present and upcoming cohorts of ethnic aged people than government-affiliated efforts will. A recent research-demonstration project (Naparstak, Biegel, and Spence 1978) has also shown the support of ethnic groups for church-run services. As a result, demonstration projects bringing local ministers into closer contact with human service agencies have been developed in Baltimore and Milwaukee.

The church would appear to be an obvious choice as an organizational auspice for many ethnic and minority aged people, but we should not automatically assume so. Among Asians, a local civic association composed of elderly individuals from the community may be most appropriate, if the members have the skills required for carrying out an organizational effort of this nature. This recommendation stems from the strong relationship between age and status in many Asian communities, which results in the elderly's often forming the core of local political and social leadership. Although this pattern has been changing as third-generation individuals begin to predominate in these communities, first- and even second-generation elderly Asians may be more receptive to services provided by the civic association than to those under other auspices. To correctly gauge the appropriate auspices for a program geared to the ethnic aged population requires that service providers have a clear understanding of the specific ethnic community they will serve.

Staff Composition

The first-generation ethnic aged person's lack of experience with individuals from other cultures may make him or her nervous or even hostile toward service providers whose backgrounds are distinctly different from his or her own. At a minimum, this tension may be expressed in language or communication difficulties between staff and clients. Even if a staff member is able to speak the client's language, there is no guarantee that he or she will evidence a comparable sensitivity to the norms and beliefs of the client.

In dealing with a number of ethnic cultures, service providers must closely match the ascribed characteristics of the client and of themselves if positive relationships are going to develop. Elderly Chinese provide one clear example of the importance of ascribed characteristics. In the Chinese community a twenty-year-old woman may not be viewed as an appropriate person to treat an elderly individual because of low status attached to a young age. In a mental health setting the ambivalence of an elderly Chinese man or woman toward a young social worker or psychiatrist may make it difficult to establish a therapeutic or working relationship. Similarly, the emphasis on *machismo* among many Latin cultures may also create difficulties for a woman working with an older male client. A Puerto Rican male may resent the idea of receiving advice on how to handle his problems or take care of his health from a woman; such advice may be seen as an infringement on his manhood.

Discussions of Puerto Rican and Chicano culture emphasize the importance of personal relationships in these two societies. Personal relationships combined with *dignidad* are assumed by Puerto Ricans and Mexican-Americans to form the basis of positive contacts between individuals. Many Puerto Ricans have complained of not being treated with any dignity when they seek medical treatment or benefits from social service departments. A worker in a social service agency who confronts a Puerto Rican senior citizen with bureaucratic regulations and is insensitive to the client's feelings about being treated in a dignified manner may find the client becoming enraged or completely withdrawing from the interaction.

The worker needs to assess the background of the older client carefully, including the dominant values of his or her ethnic culture. Agencies should then check to see that the characteristics and attitudes of the provider provide an optimal match with those of the client. In some cases, this may mean that only black providers should be serving black clients, and only Jews should work with Jewish clients.

Staff/Client Ratios

Even if an agency can obtain staff members who have the background it deems appropriate for successful work with particular target groups of ethnic aged people, program planners must still face the complex issue of the optimal ratio of staff to clients within a particular service setting. To some degree a decision on staff/client ratios depends on the goal orientation of the particular program. A program that has as its goal the maintenance of elderly people with a variety of chronic or severe physical and/or emotional difficulties may require a high ratio of staff to clients in order to provide the necessary individualized attention. The same degree of attention may not be necessary in a program oriented to elderly people who are well.

However, the attention required by one ethnic group may reflect not only their objective needs but also their subjective feelings about the degree of attention they deserve. Zborowski's (1952) studies of responses to pain demonstrates that the willingness to tolerate pain and the attention demanded because of pain distinctly vary among major ethnic groups. Staff members in a program for senior citizens may thus find that some ethnic groups are more assertive about receiving attention and are more demanding than others.

The objective basis of professionalism may conflict at this point with the seemingly unending demands of particular ethnic groups that the service provider should become personally involved with their needs and problems. Providers who feel that this high degree of involvement is unprofessional can find their objectivity standing in the way of adequate relationships with clients.

The "correct" ratio of staff to clients is thus not simple to define. As has often been noted, the kind of training and the sensitivity of individual staff members may be more important than the actual numbers of providers. One empathetic worker may be able to take the place of three workers who are less sensitive to the needs of ethnic individuals.

Program Components

Having made decisions about appropriate auspices and adequate staff, the program developer must move on to organizing the actual components of the program. The basic elements of some programs will be set by the characteristics of the clients for whom the program is oriented. In a health maintenance program, activities such as blood pressure checks or exercise may be essential. Beyond these elements, a variety of counseling or socializing activities may be implemented. Some of these may be more relevant to particular ethnic groups than others. We can best see this if we examine health and mental health programs, two programmatic areas that are vital to the well-being of the elderly.

Health Programs

Few health programs are solely oriented to the elderly individual. In fact, an interest in geriatrics has only been a recent development among health professionals. This delayed growth of interest in the elderly is partly attributable to the antipathy of medical personnel toward the older person. A recent study (Wilhite 1975) indicated that a promised shift by nurses to better hours and increased pay did not alter their preference for serving younger age groups.

Chronic illnesses that frequently afflict the older adult are also not always amenable to cure. The physician trained to cure patients often finds the slow rehabilitation process required for elderly patients to be onerous and frustrating in terms of results. If we remember that the five most common medical problems among the elderly are arthritis, hearing impairment, vision loss, hypertension, and heart ailments, we can readily see the problems of curing. While none of these conditions can be cured in a conventional sense, therapy can enable the older individual to overcome the difficulties of physical mobility that each can produce.

Ethnic older persons who lack fluency in English and come from a lower-income background may be toward the bottom of the health professionals' list of preferred clients. Health personnel find it hard to deliver instructions about drug usage to an ethnic senior citizen. In turn, the older ethnic person may not understand an analysis of his or her physical condition.

One result of the communication problems that often develop between the ethnic aged patient and the health professional is the feeling of the latter that it will be difficult, if not impossible, to obtain the older person's compliance with medical regimens. Zola (1979) has recently questioned whether the term "compliance" does not incorrectly focus attention on attitudes or "problems" of ethnic aged people that reduce their ability or willingness to follow the prescriptions of the doctor. In contrast to this approach, Zola maintains that it is now time for the medical profession to examine their methods of prescribing, to increase their willingness to attune the methods to the diverse backgrounds of their older ethnic patients, and to spend the time that may be necessary for the patients to understand the recommended course of action.

Before a physician or other health professional can even begin to worry about the compliance of a patient with a health regimen, the patient must indicate a willingness to consult with the health professional. A study of rural elderly blacks living on the islands off the Georgia and South Carolina coasts concluded that it was going to be difficult to convince this group of aged people that traditional folk medicine could not provide the same medical assistance as a trained physician (Blake 1977).

Mental Health Programs

Mental health professionals commonly make a distinction between functional problems and those problems that have their roots in an organic condition. It has long been assumed that mental health problems among the elderly are related to organic causes. Indeed, the characterization of elderly people as senile has often in the past substituted for adequate treatment. This labeling of individuals as "senile" has probably been more extensive among ethnic aged people, especially among those whose disorientation and confusion partially result from a lack of competency in English or whose adherence to traditional cultural values is mistakenly interpreted as a symptom of organic brain disorders by mental health workers.

Functional mental disorders may be prevalent among first- and second-generation ethnic aged people who have learned to rely on relatives or friends to help them negotiate the environment that surrounds them. With the loss of these helpers through geographic moves or death, such individuals may experience depression, hypocondriasis, insomnia, or even paranoia as a symptom of emotional troubles.

Assistance in carrying out daily functions may help to alleviate some symptomatologies, but more extensive psychotherapy may be needed to treat other conditions. Mental health professionals, however, have commonly believed that psychotherapy is not effective with aged patients and that only psychotropic drugs can be utilized. This reluctance to involve older patients in therapy is especially true in the case of ethnic aged patients, who are viewed as uneducated and nonverbal. Fortunately, there is increasing evidence that therapy is effective with all age groups if it is carried out in a way that is sensitive to the cultural backgrounds of clients. This would include an understanding on the part of the therapist of the history and life experiences of various age cohorts among ethnic groups.

One of the most effective ways in which to intervene with ethnic aged people would be to incorporate ethnically based treatments into the mental health system. This has been most widely discussed in relation to Spanish-speaking clients. In Hispanic communities, *esperitistas* and *curanderos* have received attention from mental health researchers because of their continued utilization by community residents. This utilization often occurs even when professional mental health services are available.

Weclew (1975) has listed a wide variety of methods that *curanderos* utilize in their work with Mexican-American clients, including methods that are considered part of accepted mental health treatment and a number of more unconventional approaches such as massage, diet, prayer, and hypnosis. The first problem in incorporating *curanderos* and *esperitistas* into mental health services is creating awareness of their existence among mental health professionals. Even with an increased awareness of these mental health resources in the community, there is no guarantee that many mental health professionals will find the utilization of *curanderos* acceptable. Service providers who are not trained in conventional mental health programs may seem inappropriate to many professionals. For these psychologists, psychiatrists, and social workers, the use of *esperitistas* may also pose threats to their previously unquestioned control of the treatment process.

The first- and second-generation ethnic aged raised in traditional cultures may be more sensitive to the use of traditional mental health resources than other groups. Their strong involvement in traditional Latin culture may make them more receptive to the types of treatment prescribed by the *curanderos* than to the often more objective and impersonal efforts of mental health professionals.

Specific Programs for the Aged Population

It is difficult to outline the elements that need to be included in programs specifically designed for ethnic aged people, since these programs are now so numerous and diverse. There are, however, commonalities among the varied community-based approaches for the elderly such as senior centers, day-care programs, and nutrition programs. All of these efforts, whatever their particular target population, have as one of their goals the continued involvement of the older individual in a network of relationships with other individuals and the community.

In many cases the older person cannot be involved with long-term friends since many of these individuals have already died.

The senior center or day-care center offers the aged person the opportunity to develop friendships with a variety of new acquaintances. If a conducive atmosphere exists, these centers also allow the individual to carry through the important psychological processes associated with aging, including maintenance or reestablishment of his or her sense of worth and a positive valuation of his or her previous years. To accomplish any of this requires the older person attending the senior center, adult day-care center, or nutrition program to have a feeling that the environment around him or her is supportive of interaction and exchanges with others.

For ethnic aged people, such an environment may be one in which the other clients and/or staff are from the same ethnic background. If it is impossible to locate a senior center in specific ethnic neighborhoods, the program can utilize components that indicate at least an acceptance of the importance of ethnic cultures. One of these elements is the preparation of ethnic foods, which the Krause study (1978) indicated was still important to ethnic women from three generations. A second component is the observance of ethnic festivals and holidays, an activity that may help multiethnic populations in a senior center gain a better understanding of each other's cultures. Discussions of life experiences may also help ethnic elderly people gain an appreciation of the common problems that each group has experienced. If these efforts are successful, older members of ethnic groups will begin to engage in the kind of life review that Butler (1975) has classified as important in the aging process. They may form new friendships and may not feel as dependent on the family for assistance.

It is possible, however, that many ethnic aged people may only derive the fullest benefit from community-based programs that cater exclusively to members of their own group. They may be unable to feel comfortable in life-review and group enterprises which involve individuals who they feel will not understand the culture and backgrounds from which they come.

Myerhoff (1978) has described a community of elderly Jews living in a poor isolated urban area in California who are making efforts to renew their ethnic culture away from the influence of the larger American society and the hostility of their children. In terms of social-psychological theory, these individuals are now able to interact with peers whose judgment about their personality and behavior stems from comparable cultural bases.

The senior center or community-based organization offers the older person a social arena in which to reevaluate his or her self-identity or to reestablish it on new grounds. Cuellar (1978) found this to be a major focus of the activities at a senior center serving Mexican-Americans. These older men and women, whose status had changed drastically as a result of retirement, were establishing new roles for themselves within the culture of the senior center. For example, an older Mexican-American could now be valued for his ability as a poet rather than for working on a farm, and such new characteristics could become a major part of the individual's personal and social identity.

In more institutional settings such as nursing homes, chronic care facilities, or even congregate housing situations, the same issues may require attention as the elderly interact in a variety of activities. Indeed, the problems that service providers may encounter in serving the ethnic aged clientele within a senior center may be multiplied in these residential facilities because of the forced intimacy they require. Personal habits such as neatness or acceptance of housekeeping responsibilities may create problems among roommates in a nursing home or in a shared apartment in a specially designed housing development. In these environments meals may be a major focus of an individual's daily life. The problems of satisfying the different culinary tastes of various ethnic groups may create problems for the staff and tensions among the residents.

Community Support Networks

So far our discussion has centered around formal services and neglected two major alternative approaches: assistance to aged people provided by other older persons, and assistance provided by family members. Biegel and Sherman (1979) and Collins and Pancoast (1976) clearly indicate the existence of important support networks in the community. These support networks revolve around individuals who can be termed "natural helpers," that is, individuals who have no formal training but because of their interest and expertise are able to provide assistance to others in the community. Natural helpers may tell a person where he or she can get help for a problem, or utilize their own contacts to solve a personal or family problem. Valle and Mendoz (1978) have detailed a *servidor* system among older Latinos in San Diego that referred older community residents to agencies and specific personnel able to meet their needs. Under the mistaken belief that urban neighborhoods are disorganized, researchers have often overlooked the existence of these natural helpers.

During the 1970s the concept of older persons' serving as supports for others became a topic of concern. In Pennsylvania, Barg and Hirsch (1972) found the idea of utilizing older individuals to interview and work with other elderly people a valid but difficult concept to implement. Faulkner's (1975) work in New Jersey also indicates that the idea of developing informal support networks among low-income aged blacks is easier said than done. Strenuous door-to-door activity that might characterize an outreach program was beyond the physical stamina of many older persons (Barg and Hirsch 1972), and Faulkner noted that many low-income aged blacks were afraid to venture into strange buildings.

Even if older workers can be hired for jobs that are not overtaxing or perceived as dangerous, many ethnic elderly people will not be satisfied unless they are served by professional staff. In these cases, the professional cannot downplay sensitivity to ethnic concerns. Programs being run under ACTION and a variety of other efforts, including the "neighborhood family" in Miami (Ross 1975) and volunteer programs in Kansas City (Payne 1977), are beginning to clarify both the degree to which the elderly can provide concrete services for individuals from the same group and the most appropriate division of labor between these natural helpers and professionals. A current AoA project in Milwaukee (Naparstek and Friday, n.d.) is also dedicated to clarifying the factors related to ethnicity that affect the development of stronger links between the ethnic elderly population and formal service providers.

Family Assistance to the Ethnic Aged Population

Processes of Seeking Help

The low usage rate of many services by older persons has led many providers to assume that the elderly either do nothing or cope with a problem by themselves. This was the response of over half of the local professionals and nonprofessionals interviewed in Baltimore and Milwaukee. Forty percent of the human service professionals (local social service agency staff) and school administrators in the two cities also felt the elderly did nothing or coped (Naparstek, Biegel, and Spence 1978).

This negative estimation of elderly people's response to crisis overlooks the process they utilize in making decisions about seeking help. All of the studies cited so far indicate that the first response of ethnic aged people is to attempt to care for themselves in an emergency. This response would be consonant with a feeling that it is important for the older person not to be a burden on children. When elderly individuals begin to wonder whether they can handle a situation by themselves, they then may turn to their functional network for evaluation and possible assistance.

In New York, Cantor (1979a) inquired about the functional networks of white, Spanish, and black elderly people, but did not divide the white population in her sample into ethnic groups. Since 47 percent were born overseas, we can surmise that many of them were ethnic-group members. In all three groups, a functional network able to provide assistance to the elderly was present. While a spouse was a component of the network for 30 to 40 percent of the individuals in all these groups, children, siblings, relatives, and friends were more important components. Asked who they turned to when they felt "sick or dizzy," 43 percent mentioned children, a choice that was four times higher than any other. In Milwaukee, Biegel and Sherman (1979) noted that over 71 percent of ethnic elderly people discussed a problem with family members before seeking additional help.

Role Reversal and Stability

Seeking assistance from family members does not necessarily imply role reversal, a widely discussed concept of the 1950s. In the role-reversal process parents begin to behave like children and children take on the responsibilities of being parents to their elders. The basis for this unfortunate portrayal of the family was a stereotyped view of the older adult as a dependent individual—a view that has reality for only a small portion of the older American population. Further research in the 1960s indicated that assistance is still a two-way street. Children in their thirties still require assistance from their parents as they take on such family obligations as marriage, birth of children, and purchase of a home. Older parents require assistance to deal with physical problems and reduced income levels.

Mutual Assistance

A common family pattern among the ethnic populations of the United States is one of mutual assistance among the generations. Whether the assistance flows more from younger to older generations or vice versa will be determined by the physical, emotional, and economic status of each of the generations and the norms of the culture about assistance. In Pennsylvania a large study predominantly of black elderly people attempted to determine the assistance provided by children to their parents (Seelbach 1978). It explored six "normative expectations" of children:

1. Married children should live close to parents.
2. Children should take care of their parents in whatever ways are necessary when they are sick.

3. Children should give their parents financial help.

4. If children live nearby after they grow up, they should visit their parents at least once a week.

5. Children who live at a distance should write to their parents at least once a week.

6. Adult children should feel responsible for their parents.

Beyond these expectations, a variety of activities that the child might perform for the parent were examined. These ranged from grocery shopping to accompanying the parent when he or she went to visit friends.

Older adults were more likely to express a belief in the six normative expectations than their children were. While these older adults received assistance from their families, they received more aid from a variety of other informal and formal sources. Seelbach's analysis of racial factors in adherence to the expectations or the giving of assistance revealed no significant differences among this low-income sample.

Assistance among Ethnic Whites

Among ethnic whites the present patterns of assistance remain unclear. Cohler, Lieberman, and Welch's (1976) examination of 386 middle-aged and elderly Italians, Irish, and Poles indicates that ethnicity does serve as a variable on which individuals make decisions about friends and resources. Italians, who are more likely to live in an ethnic community than Irish or Poles, tend to select their close friends from among other Italians. Poles have fewer contacts with friends than Italians or Irish.

These distinctive ethnic patterns influence the mobilization of friends as resources. If friends from the same ethnic background are available, the members of these three groups tend to rely on them rather than on friends from other ethnic groups. Of course, the presence of a large number of friends with a common ethnic background is facilitated by living within an ethnic neighborhood, a characteristic most common among Italians in the sample. In New York, intimates of white, black, and Hispanic elderly people tended not to be children or relatives but friends in the neighborhood (Cantor 1979b).

While the Chicago research demonstrates that friendship patterns are drawn along ethnic lines, the same study shows that elderly people usually rely upon relatives to provide a greater amount of assistance than friends. This pattern was also true of New York white, black, and Hispanic aged people, except in cases where friends and neighbors were able to compensate for the lack of contact of some individuals with their relatives or to assist those whose children were unable to provide more than limited assistance. Frequent interpersonal contact with relatives was a factor in making needed assistance available to family members. Among the Irish, Italians, and Poles in Chicago, three-fourths of the respondents visited with their adult children at least "a few" times each month. They also visited frequently with their own parents, who usually lived close by or at least an "easy drive" away (Cohler, Lieberman, and Welch 1976, p. 17). Almost half of the members of each group visited with their siblings at least a few times each month, and maintained even more frequent contact with children.

Cohler, Lieberman, and Welch also noted that increased contact on the part of the Irish, Italians, and Poles was linked to the use of other relatives or friends as resources, especially among Italian men. Given equal contact with relatives and friends, Italian men tended to rely on their relatives. The same pattern was found among Polish women. Among women in all three groups, increased contact with adult offspring produced a reliance on children rather than on other relatives or friends for assistance in problem situations. In cases where adult children had died or lived at a distance, friends and neighbors played an important role in providing assistance to the elderly.

Assistance among Whites, Blacks, and Hispanics

Similar patterns of assistance from children to older adults were found in Bengtson's (1979) study of whites, blacks, and Hispanics in California and in Cantor's research (1979a, 1979b) with the same three groups in New York City. These studies indicated that a substantial number of children were able to provide assistance to black and Hispanic aged people. This extensive resource may reflect the large number of nonwhite elderly people who live with adult children. This residence pattern results not only from the elderly's moving in with children, but also from children's coming to live with older parents who have larger homes. Mindel (1979) has shown that the number of elderly people living in intergenerational households has been consistently declining. Despite this, 34 percent of males and 32 percent of females over sixty-five were living with kin in 1977. Unfortunately, Mindel fails to provide a breakdown of these percentages by ethnic background.

Whether white, black, or Hispanic elderly people have more supportive family relationships is as yet unclear. Studies in the early 1970s (Jackson 1971; Lopata 1973; Rubenstein 1971) did not indicate major differentials in visiting patterns among the three groups. In Cantor's work in New York (1979a, 1979b), elderly

Hispanics were found to have a great potential for support because of a large number of children prepared to provide assistance. Elderly Hispanics reported a greater sense of closeness with adult children than either of the other two groups did. What was most surprising to Cantor was the lack of similar findings among blacks. As she sums up her data, however:

> Both black and Hispanic elderly are more likely to be involved in the lives of their children than are the white elderly. This higher level of total assistance probably reflects both the greater presence of the extended family in the Hispanic community and the greater need among low-income minority groups for intergenerational assistance as a means of offsetting the effects of poverty and discrimination. (1979b, p. 169)

Pichado, however, is less sanguine about the role of the extended family in the Hispanic community. From his perspective, changing technology has reduced the value and numbers of extended family units living together. The result of this change in living patterns results in a "dissolution of the kinship ties that bind the elderly to their families" (1977, p. 51), and makes it more difficult for older Hispanic people to rely on family members for assistance.

At present it is difficult to find any consensus on the contacts and assistance between children and the elderly in many ethnic groups. Babchuk and Longino's (1979) study of elderly people in a public housing project found more primary ties among whites than among blacks. In southern Virginia, researchers (Kernodle and Kernodle 1979) found that blacks had more contacts with their children than whites. The Kernodles interviewed participants in a variety of senior centers and congregate programs. The strongest primary relationships were maintained by the higher-class blacks in the sample, and the weakest by the lower-class whites.

The family also remains a major component in assistance patterns of Asian-Americans. In San Diego, a majority of elderly Chinese and Japanese indicated they would turn to their families if they needed help (Cheng 1978; Ishizuka 1978). As is true of many of the ethnic groups, assistance for maintaining the elderly in their own homes is vital, since many ethnic families have a strong belief that older relatives should remain in their own homes. Among Oriental cultures this belief is enhanced by "filial piety," defined by Wu as "the principle that parents should suffer neither want nor sorrow" (1975, p. 24). Filial piety also implies that children are obliged to provide a variety of supportive services for parents. Placing a parent in a nursing home may be seen as a violation of filial piety and may be censured by the community (Nagano 1977).

The Meaning of Family

As the attitudes of Asian-Americans indicate, the cultural characteristics that ethnic groups bring with them from Asia, Africa, or Europe must be considered in any analysis of family assistance patterns. For example, there was never any pretense that Jews were part of the many societies in which they lived before emigrating. In Russia Jews were forced to live in special areas that came to be known as the pale. For elderly Jews living in the pale, assistance was something that had to be provided by their own community. Reinforcing this was the biblical injunction that giving was a blessing. As Kutzik (1967) has shown, philanthropy was often used by the Jewish community as a measure of an individual's worth. Philanthropy has remained an important element in Jewish-American life.

For Poles, an increase in status was not a matter of individual achievement but was represented by the success of the total family unit. The individual who disgraced himself by his behavior also cast disgrace on the whole family. A basic obligation of family membership among Polish-Americans has thus been the contribution that children or spouses make to the welfare of the family (Lopata 1976). Finestone's (1964) analysis of this emphasis among a group of Polish-Americans in Chicago showed this expectation to be true whether parents were low- or middle-income people.

The emphasis on familial assistance has thus been maintained by many ethnic groups since their emigration from Europe. The result of this emphasis is the adoption of a pattern of closely knit relationships that extends even into leisure-time activities. In 1971 Coles and Erickson encountered a fourth-generation Polish-American who stated: "Mostly we see my family and my wife's family on the weekends, so there's no time to spend doing anything else" (p. 43). While this comment may be common among middle-aged Polish-Americans, the opposite complaint is often made by older Poles, who view the amount of time their children spend with them as inadequate and consequently feel abandoned.

Discrimination and Family Assistance

Discrimination has also been a factor in assistance patterns among ethnic groups. Ethnic people arriving in the United States often found service providers unprepared or uninterested in assisting them. This left them with two choices: to set up their own social and health service system, or to learn to rely on their personal and familial resources. The Jews provide the most visible evidence of an ethnic group that successfully organized its own social and health delivery systems.

Other groups facing even more overt discrimination turned to the family as a supportive mechanism. Dancy (1977) has pointed to this use of family support in his analysis of the position of the older person in the black family:

> A sense of cohesiveness is a strength of the black family, and an elderly person is often the focal point of that cohesiveness. One consequence of discrimination is that it has caused blacks to depend on each other and to distrust the dominant society which would not accord them respect. The desire for dignity and freedom from oppression helps account for the black elderly person's reliance on the strong family bond. In addition, as Hobart C. Jackson, a black gerontologist, has pointed out, economic hardship has resulted in more closely knit family ties, and the minority elderly in general usually have more family members and non-family members living with them than do their white counterparts. (1977, p. 21)

Many multigenerational black families are headed by adults over sixty-five. In 1978, 40 percent of black families headed by persons over sixty-five had children under eighteen residing with them. This contrasts with 10 percent of white families. In the black community older relatives often take children into their home rather than move into their children's household. This arrangement is possible because in 1977 "70 percent of all black families headed by elderly persons owned their homes . . ." (Hill 1978, p. 4).

Wylie (1971) has argued that among blacks, intergenerational support is rooted in African traditions. Rather than being disrupted, traditions of assistance and respect for elders were strengthened by the common suffering resulting from slavery in the United States. This does not mean that assistance patterns among all black families are necessarily equal in terms of quantity or quality. Jackson (1971) found that black parents from nonmanual work backgrounds were more likely to receive aid from children, and more often from daughters than from sons. Socioeconomic factors and family structure and relationships may thus create differences in patterns of assistance. We must take into account the role of class, historical background, and cultural changes among ethnic groups living in the United States in explaining the existence and forms of assistance that are provided intergenerationally among ethnic groups.

Ultimate Service Responsibilities

Although the family is a source of assistance to the ethnic aged population, these elderly people do not automatically spurn formal services. In Los Angeles, a high percentage of blacks, Mexican-Americans, and whites reportedly placed the responsibility for providing health care, transportation, and housing on the federal government. The percentage seeing the government as responsible for services was highest among Mexican-Americans and blacks (Bengtson 1979). Mexican-Americans in San Diego (Valle and Mendoza 1978) also saw the government as the optimal provider of programs for the elderly, although, as already noted, many ethnic elderly persons may prefer to have specific services run under alternative auspices.

Many ethnic aged people may also prefer to go to local professionals after the seriousness of a problem has been evaluated by family members (Fandetti and Gelfand 1978). A judgment by the neighborhood-based family doctor or clergyman that a problem is serious will in many cases encourage the older individual to utilize more specialized services. In Milwaukee, Biegel and Sherman (1979) found that referral to an agency by a doctor or clergyman increased the willingness of 60 percent of their sample to utilize services.

There thus appears to be no inherent reason that ethnic aged people should not increasingly use services and programs. A greater attention to issues noted in this chapter and a concentrated effort to develop links between formal programs and informal assistance networks provided in the community by family and friends could reduce negative attitudes toward formal services.

A number of results from use of services on a more extensive basis by ethnic aged people are possible. Initially we would hope to find an improvement in such individuals' health and mental health status. A wide gamut of services for the elderly are now available. Increased utilization of services should lessen the burden for total care of the older relative among the family members. On the other hand, use of formal services may create a new dependency on the service provider. This dependency could also take root among the older person's family as they begin to understand that services that can provide quality care for their relatives are available. At worst, family members could turn to increased use of institutional facilities such as nursing homes. At best, the use of services for the older member of the ethnic family could produce an important "ripple effect" in which young generations of the family change their negative attitudes toward services and utilize them more extensively without abandoning the traditional supports they provide older persons.

It is unlikely that an increased use of services will produce changes in family structure on a short-term basis. Patterns of family assistance and support have been strong components of many ethnic cultures. The degree to which technology and socioeconomic changes among many ethnic groups are associated with more extensive use of services and a greater willingness to use institutional forms of long-term care for the elderly is a topic that we will explore in the next chapter.

Perhaps the best way to conclude a discussion of services and the aged population, however, is to restress the importance of developing the positive feeling of the ethnic aged people toward service providers while avoiding the dangers of encouraging increased passivity on the part of older individuals toward changes in their lives. These dangers were noted in a famous study of protective services (Blenkner 1974). Passivity was also found to be a predictor of both morbidity and mortality in a major study of nursing home residents in the 1970s (Tobin and Lieberman 1976). Encouraging older people to become passive through increasing their dependence on service providers may be more damaging in the long run to ethnic elderly people than their current failure to take advantage of services that are now available.

References

Babchuk, N., and Longino, C. 1979. Aging and primary relations: Racial differentials. Paper presented at the meeting of the Gerontological Society, Washington, D.C., November 1979.

Barg, S., and Hirsch, C. 1972. A successor model for community support of low-income minority group aged. *Aging and Human Development* 3: 243–53.

Bengtson, V. 1979. Ethnicity and aging: Problems and issues in current social science inquiry. In D. Gelfand and A. Kutzik (eds.), *Ethnicity and aging: theory, research and policy.* New York: Springer.

Berkman, B. 1977. Community mental health services for the elderly. *Community Mental Health Review* 3(2).

Biegel, D., and Sherman, W. 1979. Neighborhood capacity building and the ethnic aged. In D. Gelfand and A. Kutzik (eds.) *Ethnicity and Aging.* New York: Springer.

Blake, J. H. 1977. Doctor can't do me no good: Social concomitants of health care attitudes and practices among elderly blacks in isolated rural populations. In W. Watson et al. (eds.), *Health and the black aged.* Washington, D.C.: National Center on the Black Aged.

Blenkner, N., et al. 1974. *Final report: Protective services for older people.* Cleveland, Ohio: Benjamin Rose Institute.

Breton, R. 1964. Institutional completeness of ethnic communities and the personal relations of immigrants. *American Journal of Sociology* 70: 193–205.

Butler, R. 1975. *Why survive?: Being old in America.* New York: Harper and Row.

Cantor, M. 1979a. The informal support system of New York's inner city elderly: Is ethnicity a factor? In D. Gelfand and A. Kutzik (eds.), *Ethnicity and aging: theory, research and policy.* New York: Springer.

————. 1979b. Life space and social support. In T. Byerts, S. Howell, and L. Pastalan (eds.), *Environmental context of aging*. New York: Garland STP Press.

Cheng, E. 1978. *The elder Chinese*. San Diego: Center on Aging, San Diego State University.

Cohler, B., Lieberman, M., and Welch, L. 1976. Social relations and interpersonal relations among middle-aged and older Irish, Italian and Polish-American men and women. Unpublished paper.

Coles, R., and Erickson, J. 1971. *The middle Americans*. Boston: Little, Brown.

Collins, A., and Pancoast, D. 1976. *Natural helping networks: a strategy for prevention*. Washington, D.C.: National Association of Social Workers.

Comptroller General of the United States. 1977. *Report to the Congress: The Well-Being of Older People in Cleveland, Ohio*. Washington, D.C.: U.S. Government Printing Office.

Cuellar, J. 1978. El senior citizens club: The older Mexican-American in the voluntary association. In B. Myerhoff and A. Simic (eds.), *Life's career—aging*. Beverly Hills, Calif.: Sage Publications.

Dancy, J. 1977. *The black elderly*. Ann Arbor, Mich.: Institute of Gerontology.

Davis, D., et al. 1977. *Health care and the black aged: A call for radical change*. Washington, D.C.: National Caucus/Center on Black Aged, 5th Annual Conference.

Fandetti, D. and Gelfand, D. Care of the aged: Attitudes of white ethnic families. *Gerontologist* 16: 544–49.

————. 1978. Attitudes toward symptoms and services in the ethnic family and neighborhood. *American Journal of Orthopsychiatry* 48: 477–86.

Faulkner, A. 1975. The black aged as good neighbors: An experiment in volunteer service. *Gerontologist* 15: 554–59.

Finestone, H. 1964. A comparative study of reformation and recidivism among Italian and Polish adult male offenders. Unpublished Ph.D. dissertation, University of Chicago.

Gelfand, D., and Fandetti, D. 1980. Suburban and urban white ethnics: Attitudes towards care of the aged. *Gerontologist* 20: 588–94.

Guttmann, D. 1979. Use of informal and formal supports by the ethnic aged. In D. Gelfand and A. Kutzik (eds.), *Ethnicity and aging*. New York: Springer.

Hill, R. 1978. A demographic profile of the black aged. *Aging*, Nos. 287–288: 2–9.

Ishizuka, K. 1978. *The elder Japanese*. San Diego: Center on Aging, San Diego State University.

Jackson, J. J. 1971. Sex and social class variation in black aged parent-adult relationships. *Aging and Human Development* 2: 96–107.

Kernodle, R. W., and Kernodle, R. 1979. A comparison of the social networks of blacks and whites in a sample of elderly in a southern border state. Paper presented at the meeting of the Gerontological Society, Washington, D.C., November 1979.

Krause, C. 1978. *Grandmothers, mothers, and daughters*. New York: Institute on Pluralism and Group Identity.

Kutzik, A. 1967. The social basis of American Jewish philanthropy. Unpublished doctoral dissertation, Brandeis University.

Lopata, H. 1973. Social relationships of black and white women in a northern metropolis. *American Journal of Sociology* 78: 1003–1100.

———. 1976. *Polish-Americans.* Englewood Cliffs, N.J.: Prentice-Hall.

Markson, E. 1979. Ethnicity as a factor in the institutionalization of the ethnic aged. In D. Gelfand and A. Kutzik (eds.), *Ethnicity and Aging.* New York: Springer.

Mindel, C. 1979. Multigenerational family households: Recent trends and implications for the future. *Gerontologist* 19: 456–64.

Myerhoff, B. 1978. A symbol perfected in death: Continuity and ritual in the life and death of an elderly Jew. In B. Myerhoff and A. Simic (eds.), *Life's career—aging.* Beverly Hills, Calif.: Sage Publications.

Nagano, O. 1977. In *Older Americans Act: Impact on the minority elderly.* Hearing of the Subcommittee on Housing and Consumer Interest, U.S. House of Representatives. Washington, D.C.: U.S. Government Printing Office.

Naparstek, A., Biegel, D., and Spence, B. 1978. *Neighborhood and family services project community analysis data report, Vol. I.* Washington, D.C.: University of Southern California Washington Public Affairs Center.

Naparstek, A., and Friday, S. 1980. Requisites for neighborhood capacity building: The aging and human services. Administration on Aging project, University of Southern California Washington Public Affairs Center.

Payne, B. 1977. The older volunteer: Social role continuity and development. *Gerontologist* 17: 355–61.

Pichado, V. 1977. In *Older Americans Act: Impact on the minority elderly.* Hearing of the Subcommittee on Housing and Consumer Interest, U.S. House of Representatives. Washington, D.C.: U.S. Government Printing Office.

Ross, H. 1975. Low-income elderly in inner city trailer parks. *Psychiatric Annals* 5(6): 86–90.

Rubenstein, D. 1971. An examination of social participation of black and white elderly. *Aging and Human Development* 2: 172–88.

Seelbach, W. 1978. Correlates of aged parents' filial responsibility, expectations and realizations. *Family Coordinator* 27: 341–50.

Tobin, S., and Lieberman, M. 1976. *Last home for the aged.* San Francisco: Jossey-Bass.

Valle, R., and Mendoza, L. 1978. *The elder Latino.* San Diego: San Diego State University.

Weclew, R. 1975. The nature, prevalence and awareness of curanderismo. *Community Mental Health Journal* 77: 145–54.

Wilhite, M. 1975. Attitudes toward old people and quality of nursing care. Unpublished doctoral dissertation, Tulsa University.

Wu, F. 1975. Mandarin-speaking aged Chinese in the Los Angeles area. *Gerontologist* 15: 271–75.

Wylie, F. 1971. Attitudes toward aging among black Americans: Some historical perspectives. *Aging and Human Development* 2: 66–70.

Zborowski, M. 1952. Culture components in response to pain. *Journal of Social Issues* 8: 16–23.

Zola, I. K. 1979. Oh where, oh where has ethnicity gone? In D. Gelfand and A. Kutzik, *Ethnicity and aging.* New York: Springer.

Chapter

4

Assessing
Ethnicity
and
Aging

Ethnicity and Stratification

Determinants of Status

It should be apparent from the previous chapters that it is too simplistic to portray ethnic aged people as suffering from triple jeopardy because they are old, poor, and from an ethnic background. Even if our data are incomplete, social scientists should be able to delineate the place of ethnic aged people in American society and the importance of ethnicity for future generations. Bengtson's (1979) use of stratification theory is an important start toward supplying a framework for a more sophisticated approach to our study. As Bengtson and other theorists have outlined, stratification is the process by which individuals and groups are placed in a status hierarchy in the society. The placement of individuals and groups in this hierarchy determines their status—a set of rights and obligations.

The place of the individual in a status hierarchy may vary from society to society, depending on the characteristics that a society uses for evaluation. At one extreme are societies that base their entire status hierarchy on "ascription," the unchanging characteristics with which an individual is born. These may include height, skin color, family descent, age, or even caste. In contrast are societies in which none of these characteristics is utilized. Instead, only what an individual can achieve is accorded any significance. As Max Weber pointed out, the two extremes are "ideal types" and probably do not conform to the reality of any existing society.

We cannot neatly place the United States in either of these polar categories, but we can acknowledge that it utilizes both ascription and achievement to determine status. The use of both categories reflects American values and the demands of an industrialized country. We can best see this if we examine status in both traditional and modernizing societies.

Status in Traditional Societies

In a traditional society, patterns of family life and survival are firmly established through the generations. Individuals born into a farming family help out when they are children and possibly become owners of the farm if they are next in line of descent. The family's life is based on communal efforts to survive, and the concept of higher social mobility for each succeeding generation is not common. Aged individuals in high-status families assume that the rights and privileges they possess will be passed on to their children.

Societies often legitimatize a strongly hierarchical ascriptive society with religious doctrine. This is true of the caste system in India, which remains influential despite its official abolition in the late 1940s.

With the onset of urbanization, many of the firmly embedded norms of traditional societies become shaky. The growth of cities offers opportunities for individuals to move away and adopt new careers. The growing labor-intensive industries that often accompany urbanization find ample use for these newcomers.

Status in Modernizing Societies

While modernization offers an individual opportunities to alter his or her life, it is at the same time a threat to the basic social organization of the society. This threat extends to the intensive relationships among the family as well as to the high value placed on age. In the traditional society, the older person is valued because of his or her experience with farming and the knowledge he or she can pass on. In the urban, industrialized society, the highest values are placed on education, recent training, and dexterity with machines. As Cowgill and Holmes (1972) found, modernization has reduced the status of the elderly in many societies. The ascriptive criteria associated with age in these cultures has become less important than the achieved background needed to assist the burgeoning development of the country.

In a multiethnic society, status patterns are sometimes based on the degree to which the values of an ethnic group resemble the values of the dominant culture. If the dominant group sees the ethnic groups' values and behaviors as similar, they may allow members of the ethnic groups opportunities to obtain social mobility despite differences in skin color or other characteristics. In contrast, discrimination may keep ethnic groups in a position where they are unable to obtain the skills necessary to achieve social mobility in an achievement-oriented society.

Social Mobility in the United States

A variety of status patterns have characterized the United States. Blacks, either brought to this country as slaves or born into servitude, were not allowed to learn to read or write. After Emancipation, southern blacks found themselves in a position of continued servitude through sharecropping and an educational system that was always separate but never equal.

Chinese and Japanese also faced discrimination in the United States after they were brought in large numbers to engage in heavy labor, especially on the railroads. However, the dominant culture has expressed a more positive attitude toward Orientals than toward blacks. In part the difference may stem from the fact that Asians were representatives of sovereign nations, even if these nations were part of the "yellow peril" that was viewed as threatening to the United States. The rise of Japan as a major industrial power following World War II and the common perception that the Japanese are hard workers and achievers has also contributed to changes in American attitudes toward Japanese-Americans.

Changing American Society and the Ethnic Aged Population

The modernization that is now in evidence in many Asian and African countries has also altered the status of ethnic aged in the United States. The immigrants who came to this country during the first period of immigration were from northern European backgrounds. In the agricultural societies from which these immigrants came, aged people occupied a position of respect and power. While the United States did not reinforce this tradition, it offered middle-aged and young immigrants a chance to find hard but often steady work. We can best understand the status of the immigrant and the place of the elderly in immigrant families by comparing the situation the immigrant family found upon arrival in the United States in the 1890s with the situation an immigrant family would find in the United States of the 1980s.

American Society in the 1890s and the 1980s

In 1890 only 3 percent of foreign-born Americans were from eastern or southern Europe (Gutman 1976). As already noted, the massive immigration from these two parts of Europe during the early 1900s provided workers for the steel mills of Gary and Cleveland, which offered job opportunities for individuals with little education and limited fluency in English. The small sweatshops of the garment district in New York provided employment for Jews, and the expanding cities enabled Italians to work beside compatriots in construction gangs. Minority groups such as Asians were still suffering discrimination in California and other areas where their job opportunities were limited to small businesses. Blacks had not yet begun to move in significant numbers to the north but remained as sharecroppers in many southern states, and Indians were attempting to adjust to the partitioning of their communal property into individual lots.

Living in the city, the new immigrant could be involved in an intensive network of family members who resided in the same area. These family members were able to provide assistance to an elderly relative when called upon to do so. Local stores oriented to the community provided familiar foods to their ethnic customers. For many of the first-generation immigrants, learning English was not only difficult but often unnecessary in the dense ethnic communities. Even the church was oriented to the ethnic community, since Catholic parishes in the United States were "nationality" parishes.

The situation that an immigrant faces upon arriving in the United States in the 1980s is extremely different. Instead of focusing on the cities, the major growth has recently been in the suburbs. Rather than a burgeoning industrial sector that demands manual labor, there is a large service and professional sector that requires individuals with advanced education. Unemployment affects 7 percent of employable workers and a significantly higher percentage of minority workers. Family members do not live in one neighborhood but instead are scattered throughout the suburbs or live in various parts of the country. Neighborhood-oriented stores have declined in numbers, and major shopping centers are located in suburban malls which can only be reached by automobile.

This movement toward a decentralized, service-oriented, educated society places extensive demands on new immigrant ethnic groups, especially those that come into the country with minimal education, expecting to make a living by manual labor. While the divergence between the structure of contemporary American society and that of immigrant groups such as the Vietnamese are readily apparent, American society has always demanded that ethnic groups adjust their culture and reshape their values to fit those of the dominant culture.

Examining nineteenth- and early twentieth-century immigrants, we find that the groups that were most rapid in their adjustment to American society were those whose culture most closely approximated Anglo values. Later immigrants from southern and eastern Europe had a more difficult time, partly because they were predominantly Catholic groups who provoked the fear of papacy among American Protestants. Extremely marginal groups such as the Jews probably benefited from their marginality, which disposed them to enter occupations not regarded as desirable by many other groups. Unlike the ethnic whites, minority groups were and are accepted slowly, and only through extensive civil rights legislation.

Current Status of Ethnic Aged People

Ethnicity, Status, and Age

As the data cited by Greeley (1974) and Roof (1979) indicate, ethnic groups in general have fared quite well in the United States. This comment must be applied primarily to ethnic whites. The major distinctions that can now be made are between white and nonwhite groups.

Excluding nonwhites from the discussion for the moment, we find it clear that the ascribed characteristics of ethnic groups are playing a less prominent role in the allocation of status within American society now than they did in 1890. Age, however, has continued to increase in importance as an identifying characteristic. Differentials in socioeconomic status between older and younger age cohorts in the United States have increased. These differentials are measurable in terms of education and training. The present generation of elderly people (from all ethnic backgrounds) has not had the advantage of the training that enables an individual to move ahead on the most prestigious career paths. This lack of training combined with stereotypes about aging has caused many Americans to associate old age with a lack of achievement, a decreased ability to learn, and a lack of understanding of technological change. From the viewpoint of exchange theory (Dowd 1980), we can see the elderly as a group with only limited resources to exchange with younger age groups. These limitations hinder older people from obtaining the rewards that are valued in American society. Unable to have a profitable exchange with younger people, the older person may interact primarily with those who share his or her limited resources—other older individuals. This pattern of interaction in turn helps to reinforce the age segregation of the society.

The lack of resources on the part of older people is attested to by Greeley's (1974) finding that variations from the mean education or income level within many groups are related to age. For the most part, older members of various ethnic groups have not attained the mean educational level for their age group as a whole. These variations are not consistent across all ethnic groups. Elderly people from Anglo-based cultures (British, German, or Scandinavian) have educational levels higher than that which is characteristic of individuals over sixty. The same is true among Jews. Southern and eastern European and minority aged people all have lower educational levels than the mean for this older age cohort, ranging from about one year less for Spanish-speaking elderly people to almost two years for elderly Poles, Slavs, and French.

Indices such as these clearly indicate that younger people in the United States have been benefiting from a variety of educational and economic opportunities that became available in the first half of this century. The G.I. Bill allowed many now middle-aged ethnic men to attend college and attain the education required for a white-collar or professional career, which in turn enabled them to attain higher socioeconomic status than their parents or grandparents had.

Status and Geographic Mobility

Many members of ethnic groups who completed college and perhaps advanced training adopted a career pattern that often required them to move geographically to maintain economic advancement. A willingness to move every few years as new and higher-paying jobs became available thus became a trait of American white-collar workers. Unfortunately, these moves separated the adult child from his or her parents, making extensive assistance to the parents more difficult.

This characterization overlooks the number of younger individuals who stayed in the ethnic community, maintaining extensive relationships with the kin network. Growing up in the inner city, these individuals never seriously considered the possibility of joining the suburban migration. How successful such ethnic communities continue to be in maintaining their attractiveness to residents is unclear. As the study by Baroni and Green (1976) shows, the absolute numbers of individuals remaining in the ethnic community is high, but the proportion of people of child-bearing age in these neighborhoods has been changing. In 1970 there was a drop in the proportion of residents in ethnic neighborhoods who were between the ages of twenty-five and forty-four, and an increase in the proportion of individuals over sixty. In ethnic neighborhoods the number of elderly people was 18 percent as opposed to an average of only 14 percent for metropolitan areas as a whole.

Ethnic neighborhoods are "graying" as younger families move to what they consider more attractive communities with superior facilities for their children. Some of these families may have moved to ethnic communities in the suburbs, but in many cases they have left their aged family members behind in the central city. Since a low income is characteristic of these ethnic aged people, they probably will not have the transportation necessary to visit many of their family members. Instead, they will be forced to rely on the interest their children have in visiting them. This picture of geographic mobility is more true of ethnic whites than of nonwhites, who have not been able to overcome the discrimination in housing that would allow them to move to suburban communities.

Current and Future Issues in Ethnicity and Aging

In order to obtain a valid perspective on the present status of ethnic groups in general and of ethnic aged people in particular, we need to focus not only on the aged themselves, but on the younger age cohorts of ethnic groups. This perspective will highlight the changes that are affecting relationships between ethnic aged people and their families and the importance of these changes for the next generation of older ethnic adults. At this point we must begin to make inferences about attitudinal and behavioral changes among generations within various ethnic groups.

Ethnic Identification

One of the most basic issues in discussions of ethnicity is the identification of individuals with their ethnic group. In his study of Polish-Americans, Sandberg (1974) found a decline in identification with the Polish community among second- and third-generation Poles. Krause's (1978) findings among three generations of Italian, Polish, and Slavic women were similar (Table 3).

More important than the actual percentages in Krause's data is the consistent directionality shown by the changes from generation to generation. With each succeeding generation the measure of ethnicity shows a decline. This is true of all eleven indices and

Table 3
Significance Attached to Various Aspects of Ethnicity by Generation

Table Indicates Total Responses and Percent of "Yes" Responses

	Grandmothers		Mothers		Daughters	
	N^a	% Yes	N^a	% Yes	N^a	% Yes
1. Being Italian, Jewish, Slavic is very important to me	61	93.4	67	80.6	60	61.7
2. Feel attachment to ethnic community	62	95.2	66	80.3	59	62.7
3. Youth should learn language of origin of ethnic group	56	52.1	52	75.0	51	52.9
4. It is important to attend ethnic church (excluding Jews)	42	33.3	44	20.5	39	17.9
5. It is important to preserve ethnic holiday traditions	59	86.4	65	83.1	56	73.2
6. It is important to participate socially with others of same ethnic group	49	77.6	50	56.0	56	21.4
7. It is important to marry in same ethnic group	55	49.1	58	24.1	61	18.0
8. It is important to marry in same religion	57	78.9	62	46.8	63	27.0
9. Of all foreign countries I feel strongest tie to country of family origin or to Israel	62	69.4	66	66.7	55	60.0
10. Ethnicity never a problem	64	79.7	69	52.2	70	71.4
11. Current average ethnic index = average number of ethnic expressions and attitude of possible 20 items on tables 3 and 4		13.86		10.56		6.43

[a] Undecided responses were excluded from N.

Source: Krause 1978. Reprinted with permission from the Institute on Pluralism and Group Identity.

the composite score based on both attitudes and behaviors. In each of the generations, the highest percentage of positive responses were obtained from the statement that "being Italian, Jewish, Slavic is very important to me." The lowest percentage of positive responses related to the church as an ethnic institution. The least change among the three generations was on the issue of attachment to the country of origin or, in the case of Jews, to Israel. All of these factors thus remain important to a proportion of the ethnic population, but the proportion becomes smaller with each succeeding generation. The implication from this study is that at least the overt identification of individuals with the ethnic culture will be stronger among the present generation of ethnic elderly people than among future cohorts. In all three generations, the church, once a pillar of the ethnic community, is no longer seen as an important ethnic institution.

Ethnic Behavior

Behavioral measures utilized by Krause indicate similar changes. The most important behavior as viewed by grandmothers, mothers, and daughters in all three ethnic groups was cooking ethnic foods at home. Ethnic cooking was done by 85 percent of the grandmothers but only 58 percent of the daughters. Ninety-two percent of the grandmothers had a husband from the same ethnic background, but this was true of only 50 percent of the daughters. While 81 percent of the grandmothers spoke a European language, only 12 percent of the daughters were fluent in the ethnic groups' language of origin. Not all of these behaviors are equal in importance. It is doubtful that cooking ethnic food is as important in maintaining the ethnic culture as endogamous marriage patterns are.

Care of Aged People

Additional research on ethnic groups provides indications that changes occur in areas of concern not tapped by Krause's work, including the attitudes of ethnic groups toward caring for elderly relatives.

In a study of Poles and Italians in Baltimore, Fandetti and Gelfand (1976) probed inner-city residents' attitudes toward taking care of aged relatives and their feelings about formal service delivery systems. The fifty Italians and fifty Poles in Baltimore were working class men and women with high school educations and incomes of approximately $11,000 per year. If this population was strongly maintaining its ethnic traditions, we would expect to find a strong affirmation of the tenet that it is the responsibility of the family to care for the elderly. This is evident in the strong agreement the respondents expressed (53 percent) that the ambulatory elderly individual should live with the family rather than independently or in an institutional setting such as a nursing home.

Individuals who are chronically ill or bedridden clearly pose a more difficult problem for the family. The demands they create on family members can require an entire alteration of family life so that twenty-four-hour care can be made available. Going out in the evening or taking vacations can easily become a memory when a family faces this kind of situation. Shouldering extensive demands for care, the family may decide to turn to a number of alternatives for assistance. One may be to utilize an adult day-care center, which provides care for the elderly during the day so that family members can work. Another is to place the elderly family member in a nursing home.

From our knowledge of white and nonwhite ethnic groups in the United States, we would not expect most families to prefer long-term care in an institution for the elderly unless they had tried all other resources and proved them unsuccessful. Less than 45 percent of the Baltimore sample regarded a nursing home as the best choice for a bedridden relative, preferring to have the family provide the necessary care for the older person. The major question facing us is whether this attitude remains as strong among succeeding generations of individuals from these ethnic groups.

Generations and Care of Aged People

Analyzing the Fandetti and Gelfand (1976) data by generation reveals changes, but these changes are not necessarily consistent with what the reader might expect. As we move from the first to the third generation, we find that the percentage of individuals who favored having the bedridden elderly person live with relatives decreased. The reverse was true for ambulatory elderly people. Each succeeding generation indicated an increased preference for having healthy elderly relatives live independently (66 percent) or with relatives (34 percent).

At work here is the influence of both attitudes and resources. The decline in the proportion of individuals willing to have a bedridden elderly relative in their home may represent a change in the willingness of the third generation to take on the heavy responsibility entailed in this care-giving situation. Making a decision of this kind, however, also involves an accurate estimation of one's resources. The respondents who had incomes of over $10,000 a year had more favorable attitudes toward the independent living of ambulatory elderly people. Because of their comparatively higher income, these families would be able to contribute to the cost of the separate residence. When the elderly relative is bedridden, resources come to the forefront in a different manner: they become critical in determining whether the family is going to be able to afford to care for an individual with extensive needs. Costs may include loss of income if one spouse stays at home, medical expenses, or the cost of private nurses. On the other hand, many of these working-class families in Baltimore may not be able to afford the costs of a nursing home.

Suburban Ethnic Groups

While the Baltimore sample allows us to examine differences among first-, second-, and third-generation middle-aged ethnic whites, it does not provide a representation of second- and third-generation ethnic-group members who have achieved higher education and extensive social mobility. To generalize about the future of ethnicity and the importance of ethnic culture to the future aged population from a limited inner-city sample would be a mistake. As yet, however, our knowledge is scanty about ethnic aged people who are not living in urban ethnic neighborhoods.

Part of the reason for this lack of knowledge has been the belief that the aged will remain an inner-city population. There is no reason to believe, however, that the increased growth of suburbia that has occurred since the late 1940s has not also led to increasing numbers of elderly people living in suburban communities. A majority of the American population under sixty living in metropolitan areas now lives in the suburbs. As this population ages, the proportion of suburban-based elderly people will also increase. Ethnic aged people will undoubtedly be a significant proportion of this population.

It is difficult to locate research on the attitudes and behaviors of ethnic groups in suburban communities. A recent study in Columbia, Maryland, however, provides some preliminary indications of the impact of the move to suburbia and the role of social mobility in determining attitudes and family linkages among ethnic suburban populations (Gelfand and Fandetti 1980).

Middle-Class Ethnic People in Suburbia

In contrast to the population of Italians and Poles living in Baltimore, the Italian men who participated in the research undertaken in Columbia were highly educated. Only 20 percent of this group were not college graduates, and the average family income was over $30,000. With their higher education these individuals held managerial and professional positions, working for either the federal government or private industry in the Baltimore-Washington area.

A group with these socioeconomic characteristics does not fit the picture we tend to have of ethnic whites, and these men's patterns of interaction with relatives were also at odds with much of our previous discussion. Whether by choice or because of the demands of a career, these middle-aged men lived at a distance from their parents and siblings. Eighteen percent lived within twenty-five miles of their parents, but over 75 percent lived at least one hundred miles away and almost a third were over three hundred miles distant from their mother or father. Maintaining interaction with parents on an intensive basis was thus difficult, if not impossible. The majority of the men interviewed relied on the telephone to contact their parents at least once every other week. Over half of the sample visited their parents no more than once every two months. While they spent holidays with relatives, their day-to-day interaction was with colleagues at work or neighbors in the ethnically heterogeneous Columbia neighborhoods.

To live at a distance from relatives does not necessarily mean that one has abrogated one's filial responsibility. The suburban Columbia population expressed an even stronger feeling than the Baltimore group that the elderly relative should live with family members if he or she was ambulatory.

Although there were few first-generation Italians in the Columbia sample, differences between the second- and third-generation respondents were illuminating. While the third generation in Baltimore expressed a stronger preference than the second generation for family maintenance of bedridden elderly people in the community (69 percent vs. 56 percent), this pattern was reversed in Columbia, where the third generation preferred to house a bedridden elderly relative in a nursing home. Sixty percent of the Columbia third-generation respondents, as opposed to only 31 percent of the third-generation Baltimore respondents, favored the use of nursing homes for bedridden relatives.

This response pattern again represents a combination of attitudes and resources. Third-generation middle-class individuals such as the Italian men in Columbia view the demands of caring for an elderly relative as conflicting with their careers and preferred life-styles. This is especially true when we realize that these men are able to maintain a middle-class life-style often because their total income comes from the full-time employment of both husband and wife. A care-giving situation for an older relative that requires one spouse to remain at home would create a major financial problem for many of these families. In contrast to the Baltimore men and women, the men in Columbia had the resources to purchase nursing-home care and were prepared to utilize it.

Socioeconomic Status and Service

Given the changing living patterns and increased social mobility shown by these studies, we cannot assume that limited use of formal services will remain a distinctive pattern among future cohorts of ethnic aged people. Many of the factors that mitigate the use of services by ethnic elderly individuals may be more apparent among first-generation immigrants than among their children and grandchildren who are now moving into the category of older adults. Spokespersons for elderly blacks have thus begun to decry not the overuse of nursing homes but the unavailability of such homes for older blacks in need of intensive services.

The affluent middle-aged Italian men in Columbia, Maryland, showed no opposition to using services for disabled elderly relatives, but made a strong differentiation among the types of services and the auspices under which these services should be implemented. We have no reason to expect that as the thirty- and forty-year-olds move into their sixties, they will have any resistance to using services. What they will expect and even demand is that the services be of high quality, responsive to their needs, and treat them with personal respect. Thus, the purchase of services by middle-class elderly individuals from ethnic backgrounds should increase. As this increase begins to become apparent, providers from all disciplines will need to be aware of the relevance of particular ethnic cultures to these individuals and the extent to which changes have taken place in these ethnic cultures during the past decades.

This analysis is consistent with Cantor's (1979) emphasis on socioeconomic status as a determinant of the support provided older persons in black, Hispanic, and white families. As she sums up the current state of knowledge: "We do not know whether the decreased likelihood of assistance on the part of children as socio-economic status increases is a response to the greater financial ability of the parent to provide for his own needs, or whether it reflects the greater geographic and psychological distance often associated with upward mobility and higher social status" (p. 172).

The Process of Ethnic Change

If we return to Gordon's (1964) model, outlined in Chapter 1, we find a framework that is helpful for viewing changes that are consciously or unconsciously taking place among ethnic groups. As the reader will remember, Gordon's formulation has ethnic groups moving through a number of stages toward assimilation. Every group does not necessarily move through each stage, and assimilation is not always the final outcome. We can examine the individual stages and the degree to which various groups have completed them, are in the process of moving through them, or have refrained from shifting their behaviors or attitudes from the traditional model of the ethnic culture.

Ethnic Groups and Acculturation

The present cohort of ethnic older persons grew up in a strong ethnic culture. In many cases they lived in an ethnic neighborhood either overseas or in the United States. The proportion of second- and third-generation whites growing up in ethnic communities has declined considerably. Raising children in a nonethnic neighborhood is more difficult among minority groups because of the discrimination they encounter in purchasing a home and/or the hostility they may encounter from white neighbors.

We have already commented on the importance of the neighborhood for ethnic aged people in Chapter 3, but we need to extend the discussion to examine the effects of the neighborhood on the socialization of individuals into the ethnic culture. For the immigrant, the ethnic community initially provides a sense of security made necessary by unfamiliarity with the culture of the new country. With acculturation, the immigrant should feel more secure and less in need of the tightly knit ethnic community and its informal support networks. In fact, as has often been noted, it is the second generation that develops a hostility for the ethnic neighborhoods, seeing them as places from which to escape as they attempt to merge with mainstream American society. First-generation ethnic aged people, whose acculturation may be only minimal, may see the skills needed to survive outside the ethnic community as hard to attain, and may view life in a heterogeneous area as threatening.

Age Cohorts and Moving

The history of ethnic groups in American society is reflected in the opportunities for social and geographic mobility among various generations. We have already commented upon the expanded educational opportunities for second-generation Americans. The result of higher income and education levels is a third and fourth generation of ethnic whites with a greater number of options about how to live their later years and how to relate to their own already aged second- or first-generation parents.

One of the options is leaving the ethnic community. In 1970 Lopreato predicted a massive movement of third-generation Italian-Americans away from inner-city ethnic communities. He even argued that this movement had already begun and was being underestimated because many Italian-American males had Anglicized their names and many Italian women had married non-Italians. Lopreato believes that the move away from the ethnic community reflects a commitment among Italians to home ownership and the sense of security that many individuals associate with a stable residence.

The geographic moves by younger ethnic people means a separation from aged relatives. Even if home ownership is not valued by a middle-aged or younger ethnic person, successful careers may require moving. The patterns found among Columbia respondents reflect a change that should become more common in the future. Among some groups, such as Poles, the movement of children away from the ethnic neighborhood to the suburbs may cause elderly parents to claim that they have been abandoned (Lopata 1976).

Structural Assimilation

Existing literature does not support the idea that interaction patterns in the suburbs will be the same among ethnic groups as they were in inner-city ethnic communities (Yancey, Ericksen, and Juliani 1976). Unless the individual moves as part of an ethnic group to an ethnic enclave, he or she is likely to associate with a large number of nonethnic people. Parenti (1967) hypothesized that the movement of members of ethnic groups to the suburbs represented only a transplanting of the ethnic community, but this does not appear to be valid. What historians termed the "area of second settlement" (the area to which ethnic groups move after leaving the ethnic community) may be largely composed of ethnic compatriots. The next move, however, may be to more heterogeneous suburbs. The existence of substantial numbers of Italian-Americans in these suburbs was shown by Gelfand and Fandetti's ability to locate a sample of Italians merely by using the phone directory in Columbia, an approach that omitted Italian women who had intermarried. Dispersed residential patterns can also be found among Japanese-Americans. Examining 5000 Japanese-Americans of the second and third generations, Montero (1979) noted that 58 percent were living among other racial and ethnic groups.

Contacts with individuals in the heterogeneous community should initiate the primary interaction stressed in Gordon's model. In turn, this interaction should lead to a relatively high degree of intermarriage. If patterns of the 1940s are followed, intermarriage would occur among Catholic and Protestant groups, with Jews and nonwhite minorities remaining basically endogamous.

Parenti (1967) argued that intermarriage is more the exception than the rule, even in terms of religiously based intermarriages. Analysis of data collected in the 1960s is now providing information on two issues: (1) whether the rate of intermarriage among ethnic groups is high; and (2) whether there is any pattern to the intermarriages that are taking place. Alba's examination of intermarriage among Catholics finds it to be more extensive than Parenti would expect, but there is some variation by generation in these rates. Among the first generation, the highest rate of intermarriage is found among Germans, a group long established in this country. The lowest intermarriage rate is among Hispanics. With each succeeding generation the rate of intermarriages has increased, except among fourth-generation individuals of English descent.

We see the same findings when we examine intermarriages among Catholics according to age. In this case, the younger the person is, the more likely he or she is to intermarry, except in the case of Hispanics, a term that includes a variety of ethnic groups. Even relatively "new" immigrant groups such as Italians or eastern Europeans show an intermarriage rate of almost 70 percent in the younger age categories. The fact that these data were obtained in the 1960s may mean that intermarriage rates among Catholics are increasing. The 1960s data also showed little selective intermarriage between the "newer" immigrant groups. As Alba and Kessler conclude: "The weakness of selective intermarriages contradicts any assumption that there is a powerful ethnic factor in intermarriages and thus that considerable intermarriage will lead only to the emergence of new ethnic boundaries enclosing culturally and socially similar nationality groups" (1979, p. 1138). The major area in which intermarriage will remain low for an extended period is between whites and nonwhites, as generations of racial antagonism and prejudices block the development of primary interactions which are usually a prelude to intermarriage.

Identificational Assimilation

If intermarriage does take place, one ethnic culture may predominate, or the family may become a fusion of the individual cultures represented by each spouse. If fusion does take place, which values will be transmitted to the children becomes problematic. While we cannot answer this question as yet, Parenti (1967) has clearly seen the importance of intermarriage in his ironic comment:

Table 4
Social Assimilation Among American Catholics

Rate of Intermarriage by Generations and Age for Each Ethnic Group[a]

	First Generation	Second Generation	Third Generation	Fourth Generation	Diff.[b]
English	— (6)	— (4)	100.0 (11)	87.0 (23)	-13.0
Irish	33.3 (12)	57.5 (40)	79.1 (67)	74.4 (43)	41.1
German	55.6 (18)	77.4 (62)	59.5 (84)	75.0 (32)	19.4
French	46.7 (15)	27.1 (48)	60.7 (28)	58.8 (17)	12.1
Polish	— (5)	57.8 (90)	64.9 (37)	— (4)	7.1
Eastern European	29.4 (17)	58.3 (103)	73.3 (15)	— (4)	43.9
Italian	29.2 (24)	38.9 (239)	59.5 (37)	— (3)	30.3
Hispanic	13.2 (53)	24.0 (50)	— (6)	— (8)	14.8

	30 or under	31–40	41–50	51 or over	Diff.[c]
English	— (8)	93.8 (16)	93.8 (16)	— (4)	0.0
Irish	82.1 (28)	59.4 (64)	74.5 (47)	73.9 (23)	8.2
German	74.1 (27)	72.4 (58)	71.6 (74)	47.4 (38)	26.7
French	53.8 (26)	36.1 (36)	40.0 (30)	44.4 (18)	9.4
Polish	65.2 (23)	63.2 (38)	57.4 (54)	45.5 (22)	19.7
Eastern European	72.2 (18)	70.7 (41)	50.8 (61)	36.8 (19)	35.4
Italian	69.0 (42)	38.3 (94)	39.8 (118)	26.5 (49)	42.5
Hispanic	13.0 (23)	21.4 (56)	16.7 (24)	28.6 (14)	-15.6

Source: Reprinted by permission from Alba 1976.
[a]The base for each rate is reported in parentheses.
[b]This column reports the difference between the latest generation or youngest age cohort and the earliest generation or oldest age cohort (formulas: latest-earliest; youngest-oldest).
[c]This column reports the difference between the latest generation or youngest age cohort and the earliest generation or oldest age cohort (formulas: latest-earliest; youngest-oldest).

"Perhaps intermarriage, as a genetic integration (for the offspring), will hasten assimilation; where hate has failed, love may succeed in obliterating the ethnic" (1967, p. 424).

Studying voting patterns in the ethnic wards of Providence and Warwick, Rhode Island, Gabriel (1973) found support for Parenti's statement. He attempted to ascertain what factors were associated with a decline in ethnic identification. Testing all major socioeconomic and demographic factors including age, income, and occupation, he found that only a few stood out as important. These included intermarriage and migration to the suburbs.

The trend that may be appearing here involves two major elements. One element is the life-style preferences that draw individuals away from ethnic neighborhoods. The second is the importance the ethnic neighborhood has in helping to define what is and what is not appropriate behavior for the individual. In their Columbia study, for example, Gelfand and Fandetti found that individuals raised in ethnic neighborhoods were less willing to use nursing-home care for disabled relatives than their neighbors raised in heterogeneous communities were.

Gabriel has nicely summed up the importance of the ethnic community: "Life in the ethnic neighborhood is also likely to mean that the respondents will be more readily exposed to whatever substructures, physical or material, continue to the persistence of ethnic identifications" (1973, p. 101). One of the principal substructures will be the tradition of interaction with and care of elderly relatives within the family unit, as well as guidance on how aging individuals should adapt to retirement and growing older.

As the present generation of ethnic people are succeeded by a generation with little actual experience of living in an ethnic community, identification assimilation should increase. Many traditions associated with particular groups may be less frequently observed. At each successive stage in Gordon's model, prejudice, discrimination, and civic conflicts that have characterized relationships among ethnic groups should diminish. One obvious conclusion of these changes may be the diminished visibility of American ethnic groups. The aged population will thus be less distinguishable in terms of any ethnic background and more visible according to the physical and social statuses that older persons occupy in the United States.

The Roots of American Ethnic Groups

To assess the validity of the contention that ethnic differentiation will diminish, we must clearly understand the roots of

American ethnic groups. In a recent article on kinship, Farber (1979) differentiates two possible bases for ethnic-group affiliation: "communal" and "associational." In a communally based ethnic group, the factors crucial to maintenance are those related to interaction, particularly interaction among family members. Associationally based ethnic groups stress the persistence of "collective action rather than the peculiar functionality of the family and other communal institutions" (Farber 1979, p. 1108).

An ethnic group whose basis is associational needs churches and ethnic organizations to maintain the identification of its members with the group. These associations have been seen as the foundation for ethnic identity among Scandinavians, who tend to hold memberships in many organizations. In a sense, the link of Scandinavians with formal organizations substitutes for strong links with family members. Thus, a reluctance to utilize the family for support because of limited intimate links may create problems for the older Scandinavian with physical or emotional problems in obtaining assistance at a time when it is sorely needed (Woehrer 1978).

Communal and Associational Groups

Of course, we cannot totally dichotomize ethnic groups as purely associational or communal. Farber's (1979) research in Kansas City points to two patterns existing among Jews. One group expressed their Jewishness through the synagogue and voluntary organizations. Farber found this group living predominantly in heterogeneous communities. The segment of the Jewish population living in areas of high Jewish concentration expressed distinctive cultural patterns through strong links with their kin and friends. This latter group reflects Winch's comments about the pattern of family relationships he found among Jews in Los Angeles. Writing in the 1960s, Winch and Greer noted that family relationships among Jews are not intense because Jews live close to their family; rather, Jews live close to their families so that they can have intense family relationships.

If the communal basis of ethnic-group association is vital for the largest segment of the Jewish population, then we must carefully analyze the changing residential and attitudinal patterns of Jews for their impact on the vitality of this ethnic culture. Farber sums this up cogently:

> As young people intermarry at high rates, as they move around the country in increasing numbers, as they produce even fewer children, as they scatter residentially among non-Jews—as these things occur, intergenerational obligations should subside and kinship ties will be seen not so much as a vehicle for social continuity but as a network of personal relationships. This trend

> apparently confirms Lenski's prophecy that extensive depen-
> dence on communal ties, rather than on associational ones,
> makes the persistence of the Jewish subculture highly vulnerable
> to environmental influences. (1979, p. 1120)

Farber's warning is applicable to many other groups and raises questions about the future of aged people in various ethnic cultures.

The Reality of Ethnicity

As other traditional values in American society have become attenuated, we have adopted a dangerous tendency to roman-
ticize ethnic heritage and the living patterns of ethnic aged people.
One common approach to Chicano families "portrays an environment in which growing old takes place in the midst of a warm and
supportive group of children and grandchildren steeped in an ideol-
ogy of family solidarity and filial piety" (Cuellar 1978, p. 205). This
picture has no more accuracy than a portrayal of all elderly Chicanos
as isolated and in poverty, without any useful purpose to their lives
and totally dependent on others for survival.

Although this volume has attempted to define what may be
termed modal characteristics of ethnic elderly people, it should be
evident that living patterns of such people are widely varied. It would
be a mistake to assume that any one living pattern will predominate
among the ethnic elderly population. We can see this clearly if we
again utilize Mexican-Americans as an example. Alvarez and Bean
(1976) have attempted to make a strong distinction between obligations and preferences of ethnic families. Thus, the tradition of families including elderly relatives living in an extended family situation
may have been adopted by Mexican-Americans because they were
unable to afford other living arrangements (as was true of Poles and
Italians in Baltimore), including subsidizing the elderly in independent apartments or placing them in costly nursing homes. As the
material conditions of Mexican-Americans improve, a preference to
live independently of their elderly relatives could become more
apparent.

Whatever the attitudes of adult children, many older
people prefer independent living, a fact that is reflected in recent
figures which show independent living by older adults to be rapidly
increasing (Glick 1979). Jackson (1975) has noted the desire of
elderly blacks for "intimacy at a distance" from their relatives. Cuellar (1978) found the same sentiment among older Mexican-Americans at a senior center in California, a feeling he attributes in part to a
culturally based belief that older persons should live apart from their
children.

Informal Support Network and Ethnic Aged

If this belief is strong among Chicanos, then a total stress on informal support systems in which the family occupies a central role in providing an older person with assistance may be less relevant to the ethnic aged population in the future. Even in 1972, Crouch found that the predominant feeling among Chicanos was that assistance for the older person should come from the government, not the family. This sentiment has also been noted among elderly blacks (McCaslin and Calvert 1975). Later in the decade Cuellar found the same feeling predominant among a separate group of Mexican-American senior citizens. While researchers might have expected the church to be important, many of the old people in Crouch's study expressed resentment against the church for not being more active in providing assistance to the community.

Informal support networks may thus continue to be important for the elderly, but will be especially valuable for those who live in cohesive ethnic communities that are characterized by intensive primary interaction patterns. Among suburban populations, where social support networks have been shown to be weaker and where the residents live at a greater distance from their families, informal support networks may not have the same meaning for ethnic aged people.

Ethnicity and Explanation

Even if informal support networks become less viable for many ethnic elderly people, ethnicity may increasingly serve as a factor around which political interest groups can organize. As Burgess (1978) argues, the long-simmering conflicts between French- and English-speaking Canadians are focused not around ethnic cultures but around distribution and control of jobs and political power. The disputes among the tribes in Nigeria centered around Ibo control of major governmental functions, and the same economic and political factors can be discerned in Northern Ireland. It does not appear that aged people are becoming a subculture of American society. It is also not apparent that ethnicity is going to disappear as an important element in the lives of the aged. What may change is the manner in which older individuals view their ethnic heritage, the means by which they express it, and the effect of ethnicity on interrelationships in their social networks.

To understand the changing importance of ethnicity in the lives of present and upcoming generations of aged people, we need to embark on more extensive longitudinal and cross-sectional studies with ethnicity as a prime variable. Our focus needs to be on both urban and suburban ethnic populations. A comprehensive approach will not be confined to examining ethnic older persons in these communities but should include middle-aged populations from both low- and middle-income groups. Only with this type of design can we clearly focus on the conjunction of history, culture, and class that is vital to an understanding of ethnicity and how it affects the lives of older adults.

It would be a mistake to expect an expanded research effort to indicate that ethnicity can stand by itself as an explanatory variable for the attitudes and behaviors of elderly people. As Bengtson comments: "To presume that ethnic differences are alone sufficient to understand the personal and social situation of the aged ignores tremendous variation both across ethnic boundaries and within ethnic categories" (1979, p. 24). Aged people in the United States are faced with a number of barriers to enjoying their later years. These include basic financial difficulties, chronic physical problems, difficulties in maintaining satisfying interaction with their family and friends, and a general malaise that can result from losses, including loss of the work role. All older individuals face some common psychological and physical demands with which they must contend. To this extent, we must give some credence to the famous comment of Kent (1971) that age is a leveler.

Not all older people are able to overcome the demands placed on them, and individuals attempt to meet these demands in a variety of ways. Ethnicity may thus become one of the major variables in determining the approach and the perspective an older individual may take toward problems he or she encounters. It is not, however, the only variable that the older person will consciously or unconsciously utilize in determining how to deal with major aspects of his or her life. An expanded research effort will provide us with more substantial information on exactly how important ethnicity is for diverse groups of ethnic aged persons and whether other social, economic, cultural, or psychological variables are taking precedence in the decision making of succeeding cohorts of aged citizens. A continued utilization of ethnicity as a major variable is thus vital in approaching a more complete understanding of aging.

References

Alba, R. 1976. Social assimilation among American Catholics. *American Sociological Review* 41: 1030–46.

Alba, R., and Kessler, R. 1979. Patterns of interethnic marriage among American Catholics. *Social Forces* 57: 1124–40.

Alvarez, D., and Bean, F. 1976. The Mexican-American family. In C. Mindel and R. Habenstein (eds.), *Ethnic families in America*. New York: Elsevier.

Baroni, G., and Green, G. 1976. *Who's left in the neighborhoods.* Washington, D.C.: National Center for Urban Ethnic Affairs.

Bengtson, V. 1979. Ethnicity and aging: Problems and issues in current social science inquiry. In D. Gelfand and A. Kutzik (eds.), *Ethnicity and aging.* New York: Springer.

Burgess, M. 1978. The resurgence of ethnicity: Myth or reality. *Ethnic and Racial Studies* 1: 265–85.

Cantor, M. 1979. The informal support system of New York's inner-city elderly: Is ethnicity a factor? In D. Gelfand and A. Kutzik (eds.), *Ethnicity and aging.* New York: Springer.

Cantor, M., and Johnson, J. 1978. The informal support system of the familyless elderly—Who takes over? Paper presented at the annual meeting of the Gerontological Society, Dallas, Texas, November 1978.

Cowgill, D., and Holmes, L. 1972. *Aging and modernization.* New York: Appleton-Century-Crofts.

Crouch, B. 1972. Age and institutional support: Perceptions of older Mexican-Americans. *Journal of Gerontology* 27: 524–49.

Cuellar, J. 1978. El senior citizens club. In B. Myerhoff and A. Simic (eds.), *Life's career—aging.* Beverly Hills, Calif.: Sage Publications.

Dowd, J. 1980. Exchange rates and old people. *Journal of Gerontology* 35: 596–603.

Fandetti, D., and Gelfand, D. 1976. Care of the aged: Attitudes of white ethnic families. *Gerontologist* 16: 544–49.

Farber, B. 1979. Kinship mapping among Jews in a midwestern city. *Social Forces* 57: 1107–23.

Gabriel, R. 1973. *Ethnic factor in the urban polity.* New York: MSS Information Corp.

Gelfand, D., and Fandetti, D. 1980. Suburban and white ethnics: Attitudes towards care of the aged. *Gerontologist* 20: 588–94.

Glick, P. 1979. The future marital status and living arrangements of the elderly. *Gerontologist* 19: 301–309.

Gordon, M. 1964. *Assimilation in American life.* New York: Oxford University Press.

Greeley, A. 1974. *Ethnicity: A preliminary reconnaisance.* Chicago: University of Chicago Press.

———. 1972. *That most distressful nation.* New York: Quadrangle Books.

Gutman, D. 1966. *Work, culture and society in industrializing America.* New York: Knopf.

Guttmann, D. 1979. Use of informal and formal supports by the ethnic aged. In D. Gelfand and A. Kutzik (eds.), *Ethnicity and aging.* New York: Springer.

Jackson, J. 1971. Sex and social class variations in black aged parent-adult child relationships. *Aging and Human Development* 2: 96–107.

Kent, D. 1971. The Negro aged. *Gerontologist* 11: 48–50.

Krause, C. 1978. *Grandmothers, mothers and daughters.* New York: Institute on Pluralism and Group Identity.

Lopata, H. 1976. *Polish-Americans.* Englewood Cliffs, N.J.: McGraw-Hill.

Lopreato, J. 1970. *Italian-Americans.* New York: Random House.

McCaslin, R., and Calvert, W. 1975. Social indicators in black and white: Some ethnic considerations in delivery of service to the elderly. *Journal of Gerontology* 30: 60–66.

Montero, D. 1979. Disengagement and aging among the Issei. In D. Gelfand and A. Kutzik (eds.), *Ethnicity and aging.* New York: Springer.

Parenti, M. 1967. Ethnic politics and the persistence of ethnic identification. *American Political Science Review* 61: 717–27.

Roof, W. 1979. Socioeconomic differentials among white socioreligious groups in the United States. *Social Forces* 58: 280–89.

Sandberg, N. 1974. *Ethnic identity and assimilation: The Polish-American community.* New York: Praeger.

Winch, R., and Greer, S. 1968. Urbanism, ethnicity and extended families. *Journal of Marriage and the Family* 30: 40–45.

Woehrer, C. 1978. Cultural pluralism in American families. *Family Coordinator* 27: 329–40.

Yancey, W., Ericksen, E., and Juliani, R. 1976. Emergent ethnicity: A review and reformulation. *American Sociological Review* 41: 391–403.

Index

Gordon, M., 14, 16–18, 97, 99–100, 102
Greeley, A., 13, 43, 44–45, 89
Green, G., 90
Greer, S., 103
Gutman, D., 22, 25, 88
Guttmann, D., 37, 58, 61, 62

H

Harris, M., 14, 20
Health conditions, of ethnic aged, 36–38
Health programs, 69–70
Heisel, M., 49
Help, processes of seeking, 74–75
Henry, W., 45
Herberg, W., 16
Hester Street, 26
"Hidden poverty," 35
Higham, J., 20
Hill, R., 36, 80
Hirsch, C., 73, 74
Hispanics, 5, 9, 35, 75, 76, 77–78, 90, 97, 100, 101
Hochschild, A., 40–41
Holmes, L., 86
Hunter, K., 37

I

Identificational assimilation, 100, 102
Identity, 18–20, 43
Illegal aliens, 34–35
Immigrants:
  first-generation, 19, 25, 31, 66, 91–94, 98, 100, 101
  number of, by country of last permanent residence, 6–8
Immigration, 1, 20–24
Immigration Act (1968), 23
Income levels, of ethnic aged, 35–36
Independent residences, for aged, 94, 104
Indian Reorganization Act, 29
Indochinese refugees, 9, 23, 34, 35
Industrialization, immigration and, 21–22
Interaction patterns, of ethnic aged, 46–48
Interethnic contracts, 60–61
Intergenerational change, within ethnic groups, 19–20, 60, 61, 66, 91–102

Intermarriage, 17–18, 100–102
Interracial contacts, 60–61
Interiority, 43–44
Irish Americans, 20, 21, 25, 43, 44–45, 76, 77, 101
Ishizuka, K., 36, 47, 78
Issei, 27
Italian Americans, 9–10, 13, 25–26, 38–39, 43, 44, 45, 47–48, 49, 51, 55, 61, 65–66, 76, 77, 88, 91–93, 95–97, 99, 100, 101

J

Jackson, Hobart C., 80
Jackson, J., 10, 49, 53, 104
Jackson, J. J., 12, 37, 52, 77, 80
Japanese Americans, 25, 26–28, 36, 38, 45–46, 47, 53, 78, 87, 99
Jewish Americans, 10, 13, 17, 25–26, 31, 38, 45, 48, 49, 54, 58, 61, 68, 72, 79, 88, 89, 90, 91–93, 103–104
Johnson-Reed Act, 22
Juliani, R., 45, 99

K

Kallen, H., 16, 18
Kennedy, R., 16
Kent, D., 106
Kernodle, R., 78
Kernodle, R. W., 78
Kessler, R., 100
Kiefer, C., 53
Kitano, H., 31
Kluckholn, F., 38
Koln, R., 13, 15
Korean Americans, 34, 61
Krause, C., 48–49, 52, 72, 91–92
Kutzik, A., 79
Kwan, K., 14

L

Latinos, 36, 47, 49, 73
Lieberman, M., 43–44, 45, 55, 76, 77, 82
Lieberson, S., 13
Life satisfaction, of ethnic aged, 48–51
Linn, M., 37
Living conditions, of ethnic aged, 36–38
Longevity, 2, 54–55
Longino, C., 42, 78